# FOOTPRINTS ON THE HEART

## The Caring Path to Prosperity

**Muriel Ward O'Tuel, Ph.D.**

*To Jane —*
*A caring professional*
*who makes a difference!*

*Muriel Ward O'Tuel*
*11-13-98*

Copyright © 1992 by Muriel Ward O'Tuel, Ph.D.

Library of Congress Cataloging in Publication Data

ISBN 0–939975–07–6

Published by Executive Press
806 Westchester Drive
High Point, NC 27262

Printed in the United States of America

Second Printing 1993

# *Dedication*

There are no self-made people. We all need help to grow, to achieve, to succeed, and to recover from disaster. I dedicate this book to my husband, Maxcy B. O'Tuel, who has stood by me for more than 30 years, pushing me forward to face challenges and make "impossible" dreams come true.

. . . And to the memory of our son, William B. O'Tuel, II.

# *Foreword*

It isn't often that a book with a motivational theme turns out to be an exciting piece of story telling. But there's a dynamic quality to the life of Muriel O'Tuel that is like the fascinating experience of a kid listening to his favorite teacher regaling the class with a learning adventure she had lived through.

Having known Muriel for many years, and seeing her too through the eyes of a daughter whose scholastic life had meshed with hers, have made this story of her years in the wild world of academia a thrilling one. The wide scope of her talents takes her from educator to public speaker, whose personality sparkles like sand in the sun.

Maybe you'll see yourself in this portrait, or maybe you'll remember that very special person who guided *you* through those trepidatious years of growing up, or perhaps you can be prodded into being one of the "good guys" others can look up to. This old world sure needs that.

**Mickey Spillane**

# Contents

# *Introduction*

My first name is Muriel. I like the sound of it when it's pronounced in the languid cadence of my native South. On the cultivated Southern tongue, it has a smooth flow, like molasses pouring onto hot, buttered pancakes in a warm country kitchen on a cold morning; like the lazy flow of the Pee Dee River as it slinks through the Low Country on its way to Winyah Bay.

When I was born, "Muriel Ward" was the name that went on my birth certificate, but my family did not speak with the cultivated Southern tongue. Theirs was a backwoods dialect that shortened and hardened the name into "Merle."

The distance between Merle and Muriel was the distance between ignorance and education; between high school and college; between drudgery and fulfillment. I have trodden those paths, and have earned the third syllable in my name. In the world of challenge and success in which I now walk, my name is Muriel, not Merle. There's a doctor in front of it, thanks to the Ph.D. I earned from the University of South Carolina, and the last name is O'Tuel, thanks to my marriage to a wonderful man who encouraged me to go for the doctorate, and who has been at my side throughout my career in education and speaking. If, on the sidewalks and beneath the shades of Tabor City, North Carolina, my family and old friends still call me Merle, I am comfortable. It reminds me of my roots and of the distance I have come. It helps me to remind others that they too can make that trek. This book is intended to help people chart their own paths to achievement and fulfillment.

As we stride toward success and fulfillment, we leave footprints. Some of them are visible accomplishments that we can point to with pride. Others are footprints on the heart—imprints that we have made on the lives of others. Many of those imprints may be long forgotten by us, though they may be treasured by those whose hearts hold the impressions. As we move toward the fulfillment of our dreams, our hearts will also accumulate footprints left by those who, in many ways, inspired us and boosted us toward our goals.

I first began leaving footprints in the moist black soil of coastal North Carolina, where my father was a farmer and a well-digger. For the children in my family, there were two major dates in spring: Easter and May 1. Easter was a time for spring finery, church services and colored eggs. May 1 was the date my father decreed for the taking off of shoes.

Whether it was sultry or chilly, rainy or dry, May 1 marked the beginning of barefoot season, and we children looked forward to it for weeks. It was almost a ceremonial thing. We would remove our shoes and socks and step gingerly onto the bare earth, our tender soles protesting each time they touched the smallest pebble or twig. But in time, our feet developed thick, leathery soles that defied all but the cruelest of thorns and briars.

It was with feet unshod that I walked the fields of my father's farm, feeling the soft, damp soil yield to my steps, gently pressing up between my toes, soothing them with its cool and comforting texture. I would trudge the rows of young corn and beans, sweet potatoes and strawberries, carrying water to my dad and my thirsty siblings as they labored in the sun. As I grew older I joined them in their labor. As I walked those rows, I could look back and see my footprints in the plowed ground.

Usually, by the end of day, those footprints would have been obliterated by other footprints, or by the hoof prints of mules, the tread marks of tractor tires, the shallow rut where a sack of fertilizer had been dragged across the ground, or the marks of sundry other

# Introduction

disturbances that kept the farm soil agitated until it finally birthed a crop.

But sometimes the footprints were left in special places where they remained undisturbed, and the sun would bake the ground dry and I'd go back a day or two later and my tracks would have hardened into a sort of permanence. For all I know, they may still be there. A few years ago, some archaeologists discovered footprints a prehistoric woman had left in the East African soil. Events had conspired to preserve them through the millenniums, through flood and drought, through earthquakes and volcanic eruptions. They were there—a permanent record of her passage on earth. I'd like to think that somewhere, embedded in the coastal loam of southeastern North Carolina, there are footprints I have left—mementos of my existence that will tell future archaeologists that I was there and that in some small way I made a difference.

Yet, though the wind and rain and the abrasions of change may have wiped my footprints from the surface of the earth, I am confident that I have left footprints on hearts, just as countless individuals have left footprints on my heart. These are the footprints that count. They are the evidences that someone made a difference.

I might have looked like a field without promise to many a person who saw a country bumpkin in mail-order clothes and feed-sack dresses making her way through high school and college. I had grown up in a home that cultivated the work ethic and inculcated strong moral values. But education was not a priority and, in many ways, was seen as a corrupting influence. Our home had no books and magazines other than religious publications. "Time" and "Life" and even "Progressive Farmer" carried tobacco ads, and many magazines and newspapers carried liquor ads. My parents shuddered at the thought of their daughter's being exposed to these evils.

Higher education was seen as particularly irrelevant for a girl. What good was a college degree to someone whose role in life was to bear children, wash clothes, shell beans, can fruit and vegetables, and cook meals?

But I was blessed with a hunger for knowledge and a thirst for achievement. Throughout my life, I encountered caring people who saw in me a field of potential, and were unwilling to let the field lie fallow. They cultivated what was there, and in the process left indelible footprints on my heart.

There was the first-grade teacher who left permanent footprints by opening the eyes of an insecure little girl to the wonders of learning.

There was the high-school principal who left permanent footprints by driving me to a small North Carolina college, personally interceding with the college president, and contributing $100 from his own pocket to launch me on my college career.

There was my husband, Maxcy, and his parents, who encouraged me to reach out for a master's degree, and then a doctorate.

Thanks to the efforts of these people and many others, I no longer walk the fields barefooted. I have long since acquired the habit of wearing shoes—even high heels—to work. My vocational milieu has shifted from the open field to the enclosed office; from the rural pathway to the urban street. Yet I have managed to pursue my career in small towns where you can still walk out your back door and catch a whiff of honeysuckle in the spring, pick a watermelon fresh from the patch in the summer, gather a basket of hickory nuts in the fall, and breathe the scent of wood smoke from a hog-killing in the winter. My rural upbringing has left positive imprints on my life, and I'd like to think that I have left positive imprints on other lives. That is one of the cherished rewards of the teaching profession, which I chose to pursue, which I married into, and which has been my life and love since the first day I walked into a classroom.

My life has been devoted to helping people succeed. I have worked one-on-one with children of the rural poor and with the offspring of affluent suburbanites in a prosperous state capital. I have worked with genius-level students and with learning-disabled people. I have taught in colleges, have served as a director of guidance, have worked as a school psychologist, and have worked in school administration as a director of staff development and as assistant superintendent in a district comprising 25,000 students. And I have worked with my own life, enriching it far beyond the dreams of the little farm girl who followed her parents and siblings up and down the rows of crops near Tabor City, North Carolina. Today, I pursue a rewarding career as a public speaker, passing on to audiences large and small the wisdom and experience I have gleaned through the years from the lives I touched and those that have touched mine.

Now I would like to make some footprints on your heart. I hope that as you follow the pages of this book you will be motivated to cultivate the attitudes, habits and practices that blossom into personal success.

The pathway to success will be illustrated at times by the steps I have taken in my personal march to achievement. I will also illustrate with stories about people whose paths through life have crossed and sometimes merged with mine.

Chapter One will stress the importance of awareness—awareness of the possibilities within each of us and the possibilities awaiting us if we exploit our inner potential.

In Chapter Two, we will discuss the environment in which most Americans alive today will spend the majority of their lives: the environment of the 21st century. We will talk about the requirements and opportunities for success in that environment.

Then, in Chapter Three, we'll explore a truth that has been quite manifest in my own life: There's no such thing as a self-made individual. We'll show how you can let others leave footprints on your heart—footprints that can lead you to success in the endeavors that mean the most to you.

Chapter Four will deal with the most interesting person in your life: YOU. We'll explore the different categories of human behavior so that you can see where you fit into the behavioral scheme. With that knowledge, you will be able to choose a path that offers the best chance of success. We will also help you to understand others so that your interpersonal relationships can aid you in moving toward success.

Chapter Five will stress the importance of balance in your life and show you how you can achieve it. Chapter Six will give you tips on becoming a good communicator—a vital skill in a world in which the most sought-after commodity is information. In Chapter Seven, we'll tell you what it takes to become a professional in whatever field you choose to follow.

Chapter Eight will cover a topic that many people overlook in their struggle to succeed: the principle that in order to find yourself you have to lose yourself in a cause larger than you are. That may sound like lofty moralizing, but it is a principle that has been proved in the practical world of business and professional transactions.

Chapter Nine will demonstrate the importance of goal-setting in leading you to success. We'll show how to set goals and how to make them glitter so that they form a beacon of light leading to success.

Chapter Ten explores the fascinating world of the subconscious, and shows how you can program your subconscious mind for success.

In Chapter Eleven, we'll conclude by showing you how to leave your own footprints on the hearts of the people whose lives you touch.

It's my hope that this book will energize you toward achieving the things you want to achieve in life. If a young farm girl from the coastal swamps of North Carolina can do it, so can you.

# Chapter One

# *Who Was Humpty Dumpty?*

*He who knows not but knows not that he knows not,*
  *Shun him: He is a fool.*
*He who knows not and knows that he knows not,*
  *Educate him: He is ignorant.*
*He who knows and knows not that he knows,*
  *Awaken him: He is asleep.*
*He who knows and knows that he knows,*
  *Follow him: He is wise.*

  *—Anonymous*

What Miss McGougan gave me was the gift of awareness. It's something many people go through life without acquiring. They live humdrum lives, achieving mediocrity at best, because they don't realize that something better lies within their reach.

1

Awareness is the first step on the road to success.
Without it, you cannot have goals. Without goals, you
cannot make commitments. Without commitments, you
can't put forth the effort needed to achieve success.
And where there is no effort, there is no progress.

## THE FIRST DAY

"Who was Humpty Dumpty?" asked Miss McGougan, and I
didn't know. The depth of my ignorance frightened me, and the
giggles of my town-reared classmates intimidated me.

Humpty Dumpty inhabited a world that had been totally closed
off to me during the first six years of my life. In my home, there
were no books other than religious literature. Secular newspapers
and magazines were conduits of evil, harboring advertisements for
tobacco and alcohol and corrupting forms of entertainment. We were
not permitted to see movies, for they too were channels for corruption.
There was no television at the time, but when it came along during
the '50s, Dad pronounced it verboten also.

There were no bedtime nursery tales at our house, either. Our
nightly ritual called for the reading of several verses of the Bible.
After that, Mom and Dad would deliver a long prayer in unison.
We'd all kneel on the floor and go through this religious exercise
every night before we went to bed. This continued until I left home
to go to college, and it's still a part of Dad's and Mom's life today.
Mother Goose had no place in our family circle. So I didn't know
who Humpty Dumpty was, and it almost ruined my first day of
school.

## NEITHER HEAT NOR GNATS. . . .

When the day began, I thought nothing could ruin it. It was
early September, still sweltering time in the Carolina coastal plain.

2

The air swarmed with insects spawned in the passion of spring and nurtured to maturity in the sweat of summer. Gnats were the most prolific swarmers. Tourists traversing the two-lane paved roads on the way to Myrtle Beach often were impressed by the friendliness of the natives, who were constantly waving. The tourists didn't realize that we weren't waving at them. We were fighting away the gnats.

But neither heat nor gnats nor tourist smirk could dampen the excitement of that first day of school. I had spent the summer in delicious anticipation. For as long as I could remember, I had reveled in the stories my older brothers and sisters had brought back about their adventures in the classroom and on the school grounds.

My brother Harold was a student bus driver, and he brought the big tangerine-colored vehicle home with him and parked it in our yard. I could picture myself in one of those vinyl-covered seats, books in my lap, looking and feeling very grown-up.

To send me well-groomed into the world of learning, Mama had ordered me three new dresses from Montgomery Ward. They were pretty plaid outfits, and the glorious smell of new clothes heightened the sense of excitement engendered by the bright colors.

Mama plaited my hair and dampened it with a wash cloth to simulate the sheen of a fresh shampoo. Well-scrubbed, well-coiffed and well-dressed, I strode confidently to the school bus along with Harold and my three other school-age siblings, Catherine, Brooks and Wayland.

Harold took me to the first-grade room. He could tell which one it was because my name was on a list taped to the door. When he left me in that room with the teacher and all those town kids, my confidence vanished.

# INTIMIDATED BY TABOR CITY

Tabor City is not a metropolis by any means. It sits in Columbus County, on the north side of the border between the two Carolinas.

About 35 miles away, as the crow flies, is Myrtle Beach, South Carolina, the capital of the Grand Strand, a crescent of beaches stretching for miles on both sides of the state line. Although Columbus County is 90% as large as Rhode Island, it contains, even today, fewer than 60,000 people. Whiteville, the county seat some 18 miles from Tabor City, can barely muster 5,000 souls within city limits. Yet, to me Tabor City, with its 2,400 inhabitants, was urban and intimidating.

The town girls wore frilly dresses with lacy petticoats, and suddenly my bright plaid Montgomery Ward outfit looked plain and out of place. So there I was in that room that smelled of chalk and apples and peanut butter, surrounded by well-dressed town kids and looking up at Miss McGougan.

## THE DIAGNOSTIC SURVEY

Anne Brooks McGougan was a woman of imposing stature. To a six-year-old girl just arrived from the farm, she looked as tall as the Statue of Liberty. She stalked around the classroom in her best authoritarian manner, and she began asking questions.

Years later, after I had gone to college and studied to be a teacher, I recognized what she was doing. She was taking a diagnostic survey. What kind of brood had Columbus County committed to her care and keeping this year? Who were the intelligent ones and who were the smart-alecks? Who were the slow learners and who were the sleeping beauties and Rip Van Winkles who needed only a loving touch to awaken them to a world of knowledge? And who were the super-achievers?

I watched and listened in dread as Miss McGougan made her way around the classroom. Then she was standing by my desk. Then she was looking down at me. And then she was asking the dread question.

*4*

## Who was Humpty Dumpty?

I had never heard of the guy, or of his brothers or of his sisters. The scattered giggles tormented me like swarming gnats, the burden of shame was as oppressive as the heat, and I felt the weight of every eye upon me. Each of those girls in the frilly dresses with lacy petticoats knew who Humpty Dumpty was. Each one of those boys in the bright polo shirts, the tan twill trousers and the unscuffed shoes knew who Humpty Dumpty was. Of all the kids in this classroom, only I, Muriel Ward, the little country bumpkin in the plaid dress from Montgomery Ward, was in total ignorance of this individual whose unsuspected existence had such an important bearing on the world of education.

Then the Angel of Liberty swooped to my rescue. Miss McGougan did not scold me or ridicule me, or say, "Look, class, Muriel doesn't know who Humpty Dumpty is."

My teacher did a wonderful thing. She knelt down so that she was lower than I was, and she looked up into my face.

"Don't worry," She said, "We're going to learn a lot in here this year."

# THE SWEET SMELL OF NURTURING

As she knelt, I caught a whiff of her. It was not the aroma of Chanel No. 5 or Oscar de la Renta or Anne Klein. It took me a while to place it, but I now know that it was the smell of nurturing. Years later, after Miss McGougan had become an old woman and I had obtained my doctorate and was back to savor the scenes of my childhood, I visited her again. And there was that smell. I wish I could bottle it and distribute it freely to everyone who ever has to deal with children.

Miss McGougan did more than introduce me to Humpty Dumpty. She introduced me to the wide, inviting, exciting world of learning.

The better I got to know her, the more I wanted to *be* her. I was fortunate enough to have Miss McGougan for a teacher in first and second grades. Because of her, I didn't miss a single day in school that first year. In fact, I never missed a day throughout my 12 years of public schooling.

# THE GIFT OF AWARENESS

"There is always one moment in childhood when the door opens and lets the future in," wrote Graham Greene. For me, that moment came on the first day of school when Miss McGougan gave me the gift of awareness.

It's something many people go through life without acquiring. They live humdrum lives, achieving mediocrity at best, because they don't realize that something better lies within their reach.

Awareness is the first step on the road to success. Without it, you cannot have goals. Without goals, you cannot make commitments. Without commitments, you can't put forth the effort needed to achieve success. And where there is no effort, there is no progress.

If you are not aware of opportunities, then you have no incentive to pursue them. Let me illustrate.

If you have never heard of bananas, you may be content to go through life eating nothing more exotic than sweet potatoes. You won't miss the bananas. Nevertheless, the person who has tasted a fresh, ripe banana, who has enjoyed banana pudding, banana cream pie, banana nut cake and peanut butter and banana sandwiches has lived a richer, more rewarding life. Such a person can enjoy bananas *in addition to* sweet potatoes. But before the bananas can be enjoyed, you have to know that they exist; you have to know that when you peel away the unappetizing skin, you expose a delectable piece of fruit.

To illustrate again: The person who has never heard of Shakespeare, Wordsworth or Faulkner; who has never heard of Mozart,

Beethoven or Chopin, may be content to go through life reading TV Guide or The Farmer's Almanac and listening to "On Top of Old Smokey" or "Blue Suede Shoes."

Nevertheless, the people who have learned to appreciate serious literature and classical music have added a rich, rewarding dimension to their lives. They can enjoy the Farmer's Almanac *and* Faulkner; "Blue Suede Shoes" *and* "Moonlight Sonata."

In my case, it might have been possible, during my preschool years, to absorb Humpty Dumpty and sound religious values. But I was unaware of Humpty Dumpty and all the other Mother Goose characters, so I missed out. Miss McGougan opened up my awareness.

## EXPERIENCE THE WORLD

How do you achieve awareness?

First of all, you have to look around you. Experience the world. Be willing to open yourself to new ideas and new experiences. So you're into rock music. Fine. Enjoy it. But why not go to your local library and check out an album or two of classical music? Listen to it a few times. You may develop an ear for it. Now you've broadened your awareness. You have opened yourself to an even wider range of music.

Try some other new experiences. Go to a sushi bar. Go to a French restaurant and order escargot. If you've never tried raw oysters or boiled peanuts or scrapple or squid or shark-fin soup or grits, try them—at least once.

Take a trip occasionally to some other part of the country—or even to a foreign country if you can afford it. (London is closer to the East Coast than Los Angeles. Cross a bridge in Detroit and you're in Canada. From El Paso, you can practically jump the Rio Grande into Mexico. The Caribbean is just a short hop from Miami.) If you can't afford the air fare, read some travel magazines or the travel sections of your newspaper.

Read sections of your newspaper that you don't ordinarily read. If you normally buy it for the sports section, take a look at the editorial page, the opposite-editorial page, or the business section. If you pride yourself on being a staunch conservative, read an occasional piece by a flaming liberal—not with the idea of converting to liberalism but with the idea of understanding the liberal point of view and rebutting it, if necessary. If you're a flaming liberal, take the same tack with conservative writers.

It is through this type of adventurousness that you gain an awareness of what's out there. With this awareness, you can take advantage of your opportunities.

# WINDOWS ON THE GOOD LIFE

My first ventures toward awareness were modest indeed. For a role model, I might have chosen my own mother, a woman who expressed her deep love through hard work and sacrifices for her children. She accepted Dad's family headship without audible protest, and saw that her seven surviving children (an eighth died after less than a week of life) were clean, well-fed and well-clothed. In those days, chicken feed often came in sacks made of cloth with floral patterns. Mama would take these sacks and make attractive dresses for herself and her daughters. She was the model of a dutiful, conscientious, 19th century country housewife.

But this was the 20th century, and if I was to reach my full potential, I had to have a role model from this century. The America of the 1950s and beyond would be an affluent society, and I needed a role model who was at home amid affluence.

Anne Brooks McGougan was such a role model. If Columbus County were a feudal society, Miss McGougan's family would be among the nobility. She had grown up in an atmosphere of refinement and had absorbed a tradition of service toward fellow humans. She was proud of her stratum in society, but not ashamed to reach down to help others step up from their lower strata. Miss McGougan gave me a window on the good life. I fondly gazed through it and, at the proper time, took my place comfortably and confidently on the other side.

I also obtained a window on the good life through Anne Mallard, whose father was the town's only lawyer. She and I were good friends as well as academic competitors. She beat me by a fraction of a point in the race for high-school class salutatorian (We were both edged out for valedictorian by Joanne Watts).

In cultivating Miss McGougan as a role model and Anne as a friend, I was stretching beyond the social level into which I was born. But to achieve your potential, you often have to stretch beyond your comfort level. That's how you achieve awareness; that's how you grow.

## DIFFERENT STROKES. . . .

Not everyone will stretch in the same direction; not everyone will be excited by the same opportunities. Not everybody defines success and prosperity in quite the same way. There's nothing odd about that. After all, some people have eaten bananas and can take them or leave them—even when they're in banana pudding. Some people cultivate a taste for escargot and some never get over their aversion to snails.

In the world of business, some people are motivated by accumulating a fortune. Others look for personal fulfillment. Some like to accumulate material possessions. Others like to accumulate experiences. For one person, a memorable experience might be a candlelight and wine dinner at a prestigious restaurant. For another, it might be take-out barbecue, or a picnic down by the creek.

# A NIGHTMARE IN CHARLESTON

An experience with my parents demonstrated strikingly the difference between the values I have acquired during my life and the values they have adhered to throughout theirs. It also showed how their preoccupation with the rural life had drawn around them a curtain that shielded them from enriching experiences. It kept them from gaining an awareness of many exciting possibilities that they might have exploited without compromising their religious or moral values. It happened in Charleston during graduation week-end at The Citadel, the military college of South Carolina.

We sent both our sons, William and Bryant, to The Citadel. When William's graduation day approached, I decided to have my parents down for the week-end. We were living at that time near Harleyville, a small town about 45 miles from Charleston, but the week-end was so filled with activity that we decided to stay in a hotel in town.

I wanted to make this a memorable event for Mama and Dad, so I rented several large rooms on the tenth floor of the Francis Marion Hotel, overlooking downtown Charleston and its famous Battery. I knew Mom and Dad would be uncomfortable going to restaurants; eating out was not a part of their lifestyle. For this reason, I reserved a room with a dining table and provided plenty of food.

I was quite excited over the opportunity to do this for my parents. This was their first visit to a town the size of Charleston, and I had arranged for them to take a tour of the historic old city. I could imagine their excitement.

But for Mom and Dad it was an occasion for anxiety instead of excitement. They had never ridden an elevator before. They were nervous about getting into a small room that moved up and down, pulled through a vertical shaft by cables. When they got to the tenth floor, they didn't want to look out the windows at the marvelous view of the city. They thought it was dangerous to be so high off the ground. After dinner, they decided to forgo the tour of Charleston. They just wanted to go to bed and get some rest.

Next morning, I went out for some sausage biscuits and milk for breakfast, then drove them to the campus for the graduation ceremony.

"I'm sure glad to get both my feet on the ground," said Dad. "I didn't sleep much at all. I kept thinking, 'Man, we'd be in a fix if this place caught on fire.'"

What would have been a memorable experience for "Merle" Ward turned out to be a nightmare for her aging parents. The trouble and expense had been wasted on Dad. He told me: "Look: When you come to see us, we fix you up at home and we cook good meals. When Bryant graduates, I want to stay at your home."

Had Mama and Dad been more open to awareness, the nightmare might have been a rewarding experience. Suppose they had looked out that window and been enthralled by the view of Charleston. Suppose the view had whetted their appetite for a boat trip to historic Fort Sumter, a drive to Fort Moultrie, a tour of the carrier Yorktown, a visit to the lovely old homes that grace the narrow peninsula where, as Charlestonians say, the Ashley River meets the Cooper River to form the Atlantic Ocean.

Mama's and Dad's awareness would have opened up to them newer and richer pleasures. Who knows? Today, Charleston; tomorrow, New York. Or at least Atlanta.

So to expand your awareness, look for new experiences and try new things. You may discover a delectable fruit that you never imagined could exist.

## DIFFERENT YARDSTICKS

Not everyone will measure success by the same yardstick. Some may enjoy manipulating the levers of power in a large organization.

Others may prefer individual accomplishment through creative efforts.

Some may enjoy learning, and thus devote their lives to academic achievement.

Some may be attracted to the law, and may regard success as the achievement of a great courtroom reputation.

Some may yearn to travel, and thus seek out careers that call for globe-trotting. Some may prefer to remain in the communities where they were born, rearing healthy families and making their communities better places in which to live.

Some may seek success in the financial arena, with the goals of amassing great fortunes. Others may seek greatness in the service of humanity, their objectives being Nobel prizes.

But you won't seek greatness unless you're aware that it is possible.

## A DIFFERENT ENVIRONMENT

We all adjust our attitudes and our actions to fit the environments we perceive. If we perceive an environment that is barren of opportunity, we adjust our attitudes and behavior accordingly. If we perceive an environment teeming with possibilities, we adjust our thinking and behavior to exploit them.

Note that we respond to the environment we *perceive,* and not necessarily to the real environment. Therefore, awareness, in effect, creates a new environment for us. When we become aware of the possibilities, we can begin to take advantage of them.

Let me use a fictitious example:

## LITTLE TURTLE AND THE ALLIGATOR

Little Turtle was a Seminole Indian boy captured by some of Andrew Jackson's men during Old Hickory's campaign in Florida.

# Who Was Humpty Dumpty?

On his way north, the boy escaped and eventually made it to the swamps of the Cape Fear River in North Carolina.

Hunting had been unproductive, and one day dusk found Little Turtle beside a broad stream, hungry and tired.

Across the river, he saw a vine heavy with ripe fox grapes. He was about to swim across and enjoy a sweet banquet when he discerned, in the dying sunlight, a sinister form just beneath the surface of the black water.

Little Turtle shuddered.

"If I had jumped in without looking, that alligator would have had me for dinner," he said to himself.

Little Turtle camped by the river, hoping that by morning the alligator would have moved on and he could find a safe place to cross the stream. He dared not sleep on the soft ground, lest the 'gator cross the river in search of a midnight snack. So he spent an uncomfortable night wedged into the forks of a big black gum tree, wishing the pangs of hunger would release him to sleep.

When sunlight at last warmed the river bank, Little Turtle climbed down and looked to see where the alligator had lain. The sinister-looking form still lurked beneath the water. But by the light of day, Little Turtle could see that it wasn't an alligator at all; it was just the trunk of a fallen tree. Little Turtle could also see that the water was quite shallow and could be easily forded. He crossed over and enjoyed a succulent breakfast of fox grapes.

Little Turtle had a problem of awareness. His *perceived* environment was the swamps of Florida, which were alive with dangerous alligators. His *real* environment was coastal North Carolina, where alligators are all but unknown. He *perceived* a dangerous reptile guarding the fox grape vine. In reality, the object was a harmless log. By responding to the *perceived* environment instead of to the real one, Little Turtle denied himself a comfortable night's sleep on a full stomach.

## THE SNOWBOUND MOTORIST

You've heard of other instances in which people have suffered because they responded to perceptions instead of to reality.

A motorist traveling through Minnesota during the winter was caught at nightfall in a blizzard that made the road impassable. Seeing nothing but snow everywhere he looked, he decided it would be best to stay in the car and use the heater for warmth. But he had failed to keep his fuel tank full, and the engine died during the night. So did the motorist, for he had nothing to protect him from the cold. He was found the next morning frozen to death.

His car had stalled just 100 feet from the entrance to a Holiday Inn. With electric power out, there had been no lighted sign to reveal the presence of the motel.

The motorist perceived an environment of endless snow with no shelter within reach.

His actual environment was quite hospitable: a warm motel within easy walking distance of his car.

Had he been aware of his *actual* environment, he would have shut off his engine, put on his overcoat and walked to the motel. Instead, he reacted to his *perceived* environment, and died as a result.

## THE BECKONING HALLS OF ACADEME

Had I gone through life perceiving my environment as no more than rural Columbus County, North Carolina, I would have had no incentive to go to college and earn a doctorate. I would have been ignorance-bound, though just beyond my perceived environment, the warm halls of academe would have been waiting. Unaware of them, I would have remained Merle, a nice girl who stayed home and shelled beans, cooked meals, washed and ironed, and raised children.

*14*

But early in my school life, I perceived a much wider environment. I adjusted my attitudes and my actions to fit it, and I became Muriel. Now they call me Dr. O'Tuel, and instead of shelling beans, I travel to banquets to share my knowledge and experiences with others. Those others often are people whose educational and career attainments would have placed them far beyond the field of vision of most farm girls working the soybean fields of Columbus County. I have even addressed a presidential forum in Washington, D.C., a place that to the pre-McGougan Muriel would have been as remote as another planet. Columbus County, North Carolina, is still a cherished part of my environment, but it isn't my total environment. Thank God, I acquired awareness.

## BUSH HOGS AND 'LEASTIES'

As I look back, I think of children whose lives my colleagues and I have touched and to whom we have attempted to impart the precious gift that Miss McGougan passed on to me.

I think of Jason, a youngster from Horry County, Columbus County's neighbor across the state line. He was in a kindergarten class, and the school principal had heard that both teacher and pupils were weary from the ordeal of providing structure for children who were not accustomed to being pent up in classrooms and tied down by learning tasks.

"It's been a tough week, I know," said the principal, "but the good news is that tomorrow is Saturday, and you can sleep late and watch cartoons."

The speech didn't seem to cheer Jason at all. He continued to frown and to look inconsolably bored.

The principal kindly put his arm around him.

"Tomorrow's Saturday, Jason," he said encouragingly. "What kind of exciting things do you have planned?"

"Hell," said Jason with resignation. "I reckon I'll get up and bush hog like we always do on Saturday."

It's my hope that education will open Jason to the awareness that Saturdays were not made just for clearing land with a piece of balky mechanical equipment. There are exciting possibilities for him, if he will recognize them and adjust his attitudes and actions toward achieving them.

I remember too the young lad in Dorchester County, South Carolina, whose teacher was trying to teach her charges the difference between "most" and "least."

She had a number of small toy farm animals, and she would place them in piles of different sizes: four cows over here, eight pigs over here, two chickens here.

"Is this the most or the least," she said to the farm youngster.

"Miss Gadsden," he told her, "We got chickens and pigs and cows, but we ain't got no 'leasties.' "

The youngster, I hope, has since learned the concept of most and least—and also that the world is full of fascinating things that go far beyond the South Carolina farmyard that had been his environment.

# HANDWRITING ON THE WALLS

I had my personal experience with a group of youngsters who perceived themselves in an environment of ignorance. I was teaching high-school English in Columbia, South Carolina, the year the schools were first desegregated. It was a year of turmoil, for the school-district lines had been drawn so that inner-city children were bused into this suburban school and were mixed with the offspring of affluent upper middle-class parents of both races.

One class of ninth-graders consisted almost entirely of pupils who were repeating at least one grade. In fact, I had some 18-year-olds in that ninth-grade class.

When I gave them a reading assignment, one of them told me:

*16*

"Ain't you heard? We can't read; we don't know how to do this stuff."

"I don't believe that," I said. "I'll tell you what: Let's go down the hall to the rest rooms, and you girls go into the girls' rest room and you guys into the guys' rest room. If there's any word on the wall or anywhere else in the rest room that you can't read, come back to me and I'll go in there and read it for you."

We went out of the classroom and down the hall. There wasn't a word on those walls that my students couldn't read. And if they could read words on rest-room walls, they could learn to read words on job-application forms. They could learn to read the instructions on the equipment they might have to operate on the job. They might even learn to read Dylan Thomas and Samuel Taylor Coleridge; William Faulkner and Truman Capote; James Baldwin and Alex Haley.

The point is that those students were able to read. But they had been living in a literary desert. They had been told they couldn't read, and so they *perceived* themselves as illiterate. In reality, they were quite capable of reading. They knew, but they knew not that they knew.

# DON'T COUNT YOUR CHICKENS BEFORE THEY'RE CAUGHT

If you really push your awareness, you may even perceive opportunities that aren't there—then turn them into reality.

Such was the case with my Uncle Dalton, who lived in town while we lived in the country. Uncle Dalton liked fried chicken, and it was a regular part of his menu. Now in those days (we're talking '40s and '50s in rural North Carolina) you didn't buy up a supply of frozen fryers and store them in your freezer. Who had a freezer? So Uncle Dalton would buy his chickens live from a man named Walter. At regular intervals, Walter would deliver a dozen chickens to Uncle Dalton's door.

One day Walter arrived to deliver some chickens, but Uncle Dalton wasn't home. Not wanting to disappoint a good customer, Walter left the chickens in a crate. Somehow, the chickens managed to escape before Uncle Dalton got home.

Uncle Dalton called all his kids and sent them scouring the town for loose chickens.

A few days later, Uncle Dalton saw Walter.

"Walter," he said, "I'd appreciate it if you wouldn't leave me any chickens when I'm not at home. Those you left me got out, and we were only able to round up eight of them."

"Heck, Dalton, you didn't come out so bad," drawled Walter. "I only left you six."

So sharpen your awareness of the opportunities out there. You never know how many chickens may be running loose in the bushes.

# DON'T LET LOGS SCARE YOU

You too may be a victim of your perceived environment. Like Little Turtle, you may be letting non-existent alligators scare you away from the rewards that could be yours. You need to realize that most of those "alligators" are harmless logs.

Are you letting the lack of an education scare you away from your dreams? That's a log, not an alligator. If you are a high-school student, there are many avenues for financing a college career. Consult your school guidance counselor. Write to a number of colleges— including the small ones that don't send teams to the Sugar Bowl but do offer educational opportunities and financial assistance.

Are you allowing your cultural background to hold you back? That's a log, not an alligator. Remember the kid named Lincoln, who grew up on the rough frontier, split rails and performed other menial tasks? He ended up as the host of sophisticated White House functions. His first name was Abraham.

Remember the kid named Washington, who slept on a dirt floor atop a pile of rags; who spent his childhood doing fetch-it chores for a Virginia farm family? He ended up founding a famous educational institution. His first name was Booker.

Do you see yourself as lacking in intellectual qualities? That's a log, not an alligator. Thomas Edison, Albert Einstein and Winston Churchill all were perceived as intellectual dullards in their early years. But they learned to exploit the special intelligences they possessed. You have talent that can carry you to success. Look for it. You'll usually find it in the pursuits that you enjoy most. Stretch yourself and see how you grow.

Do you see yourself as too young? That's a log, not an alligator. Being young means that you have the time and the youthful energy to accomplish your goals. Alexander the Great was the master of Western civilization by the time he was 30. John Keats produced a body of poetry worthy of literary immortality by the time of his death at the age of 26. Einstein was 26 when he propounded his Theory of Special Relativity and 35 when he produced his Theory of General Relativity.

Do you see yourself as too old? That's a log, not an alligator. Grandma Moses, Harland Sanders and many others can testify to that.

Are you physically handicapped? That's a log, not an alligator. Helen Keller could neither see, hear nor speak, but she achieved greatness. Franklin Roosevelt was crippled by polio and confined to a wheelchair. Yet he campaigned for and won the presidency of the United States—four times.

Stephen Hawking, while in his 20s, contracted an incurable neurological disease that left him almost totally incapacitated physically. Yet he became a student of the universe and propounded the theory of exploding black holes. Although he couldn't walk, or even wait on himself, he became one of the youngest people ever elected to

Britain's Royal Society and was awarded the professorship at Cambridge University once held by Sir Isaac Newton.

# THE STORY OF JEAN CATE

And let me tell you about Jean Cate of Columbia, South Carolina. I used to sit next to Jean in Park Street Baptist Church, sharing my Bible with her, going into her pocketbook when she wanted me to take out the money for her weekly church offering.

I missed her when my family moved away from Columbia, but I kept sending her our Christmas newsletter, and one day I heard from her.

"Will you ever forgive me?" she wrote. "For more than several years, now, you have remembered me at Christmas with your newsletters and cards, and every year, I keep thinking that I must write and let you know what's been happening with me. And as you know, I don't do it.

"So, now, I'm making amends and will endeavor to change my ways."

She changed her ways indeed. I recently received a copy of a novel entitled "True Identity," copyrighted in 1990 and published by Three Rivers Publishers of Columbia. The author was Jean Cate. If it never makes the best-seller lists, it still will deserve a special place in the annals of courage.

Jean Cate was born with cerebral palsy. It crippled her body, but not her mind. Jean was among the first generation of handicapped children in South Carolina to be integrated into the public schools. She graduated in 1963 from Columbia High School, determined that she would surmount her handicap and realize her full potential as a human.

For Jean Cate to become a novelist, she had to overcome an obstacle most novelists don't encounter. Her handicap makes it very difficult for her to control speech or hand movements. So she had to type the entire manuscript by using a device strapped to her head. She could not use the "touch system" on the typing keyboard that ordinary novelists can master. She had to pick out the letters painstakingly, one at a time.

Yet she felt called upon to seek my forgiveness for failure to respond to my cards and newsletters. Jean Cate has a handicap. But it's a feeble impediment, indeed, compared to the power she summoned in her heart and mind. Hers was the sweet satisfaction mentioned in this poem that I keep handy for reading when the going gets tough:

> There is no thrill in easy sailing,
> When skies are clear and blue;
> There's no joy in merely doing
> Things which anyone can do.
> But there is great satisfaction
> That is mighty sweet to take,
> When you reach a destination
> People thought you'd never make.

## GO FOR SUCCESS

Like the Minnesota motorist, you may give up when success is within easy reach, because you can't actually see it. Learn to see success in your mind's eye. And go for it.

Like the youngster whose Saturdays were spent bush-hogging, you may feel trapped in a routine that is familiar but boring. Look around you. It's a big world, full of stimulating things to do. Find them and do them.

Like the child who had never seen any "leasties," your imagination may be hemmed in by the boundaries of the familiar. Go out and explore. The unknown world is full of pleasant surprises.

Like the students who thought they couldn't read, you may be saddled with a feeling of inadequacy. Don't fall into that trap. Let me share with you a poem by R. L. Sharpe that I memorized in Nettie B. Hammond's sixth-grade class in Tabor City:

## A BAG OF TOOLS

Isn't it strange
That princes and kings
And clowns that caper
In sawdust rings,
And common people
Like you and me
Are builders for eternity?

To each is given
A bag of tools,
A shapeless mass,
A book of rules;
And each must fashion,
Ere life is flown,
A stumbling block
Or a steppingstone.

You can do a great deal more than you give yourself credit for. Take on a few tasks you think are just beyond you. Go in with a determination to master them. You'll be surprised at how good you are.

Now look ahead. The 21st century is just on the horizon. It will offer exciting opportunities for those who want to seize them.

Let's move to the next chapter for a view of what lies ahead.

# Chapter Two
## *Success Beyond 2000*

*Look not mournfully into the Past. It comes not back again. Wisely improve the Present. It is thine! Go forth to meet the shadowy Future, without fear, and with a manly heart.*
*—HENRY WADSWORTH LONGFELLOW*

As this book is written, human knowledge is doubling about every six years. By the turn of the century, it will be doubling about every 32 hours, as mankind continues its computerized exploration of the universe.

That means that those of us who experience the turn of the century will have to prepare ourselves for unprecedented change. The skills many of us have cultivated in this century will be about as useful in the next as the ability to guide a mule down a straight furrow.

# FROM GEE-HAW TO JETLINER

I have plowed behind a mule and I have flown aboard a jetliner. In a sense, the story of my life has been the story of the 20th century. By mid-century, the farm mule was obsolete. I have no doubt that by the middle of the 21st century the jetliner will have become obsolete. Those who succeeded in the 20th century had to change with the times. Those who succeed in the 21st century will have to change too—but a lot faster.

To go back to the mule and me. It was a short and not very successful experience, but I remember it well.

I would watch my father and my brothers follow the mule back and forth across the field, creating arrow-straight furrows. Sometimes I'd follow them, enjoying the feel and smell of the fresh earth as they plodded behind the big animal, singing out a chorus of "gee there . . . now haw . . . whoa there. . . . now giddyap!"

One day I begged my dad to let me try it. He finally gave in. I took hold of the ropes that were attached to the mule's bridle and held one in each hand while I gripped the wooden handles of the plow.

"Giddyap," I commanded.

The mule leaned forward, the trace chains lost their slack, and the blade of the plow bit into the soil. But it wouldn't go straight. The plow wobbled from left to right, and I didn't have the strength or the skill to plow a straight furrow. Fortunately, my success in life did not depend upon my ability to plow with a mule.

# A 19TH CENTURY SKILL

My brothers were good at it, but even for them, a mule-drawn plow did not cut a furrow to success. That kind of plowing was a 19th century skill that hung on into the 20th century and died a peaceful death sometime during my life. I'm not sure exactly when it happened. I know that when my Uncle Thomas died in 1955, his widow, Aunt Bert, wanted Dad to sell the mule he left her. Dad was unable to make the sale and Aunt Bert never forgave him. I suppose that means that by mid-century, mules were excess baggage on most farms and there was no longer a market for them. I do know that when I go back to Tabor City, I no longer see one-horse and two-horse plows working the corn, tobacco and soybean fields.

My sister Anne married Furnie Hughes, a struggling farmer who was quite familiar with the hind quarters of a mule, having plowed behind many a long-eared beast. But now Furnie is one of the most prosperous farmers in Columbus County. He didn't get that way by learning the best way to plow a mule. He achieved prosperity by following the latest trends in agricultural technology. He owns a diversified 750 acre farming operation that includes 120 acres of tobacco, and he has at least one piece of equipment that probably cost more than my home. And with built-in air conditioning and stereo, it's darned near as comfortable.

So the mule is gone. No more do we see mule-drawn wagons hauling produce into town. No longer do we see the occasional horse-drawn buggy drawn up to a country store. As a matter of fact, you don't see too many country stores. They've been replaced by 7-Elevens, Handy Pantrys, Quik-Stops, Hop-Ins and a host of other convenience stores that belong to regional or national chains.

At some point, when I was no longer looking, a way of life vanished in the smoke and fire of the 20th century. We rarely speak of a "way of life" any more. We speak of "lifestyles," which usually don't stay around long enough to become ways of life.

It's as if the 20th century threw time into passing gear, and we've been accelerating at a dizzying pace ever since the first horseless carriage scattered the chickens in a farm yard; ever since the Wright Brothers strapped a motor to a large kite at Kitty Hawk and went aloft in it.

Barring an unforeseen global catastrophe, we aren't likely to slow down in the 21st century. As this book is written, human knowledge is doubling about every six years. By the turn of the century, it will be doubling about every 32 hours, as mankind continues its computerized exploration of the universe. The world will have changed more between 1990 and 2000 than it did between 900 A.D. and A.D.

That means that those of us who experience the turn of the century will have to prepare ourselves for unprecedented change. As steam, electricity and internal combustion supplied the muscle formerly supplied by the human back, so the robot will provide the dexterity formerly supplied by the human hand. In 1982, there were 32,000 robots to do the bidding of their human masters in the United States. By 1989, there were 1.3 million, and by 1995 the number was expected to exceed 20 million. The skills many of us have cultivated in this century will be about as useful in the next as the ability to guide a mule down a straight furrow.

The computer will free the human mind from the drudgery of rote tasks and free it to imagine and to innovate. Simple literacy will no longer suffice. Computer literacy will be essential, and advanced education will be a particular asset. College graduates will earn 43% more than people with high-school diplomas.

Those who ignore the impacts of the robot and the computer may be shocked at the kinds of jobs available to them in the 21st century. The 20th century saw a dramatic shift in employment from agriculture to production. In 1900, it took 85% of the American work force to man the agricultural jobs necessary to feed a nation of 76 million people. In 1989, only 3% of us worked on the farm, but that 3% produced twice as much food as 250 million Americans could eat. Exit the farm hand. Agriculture became automated, and farm jobs disappeared. To replace these farm jobs, American industry came to life and produced production jobs. By 1950, 73% of Americans were employed in production and manufacturing. By 1989, that percentage had dropped to somewhere between 15% and 21%. Exit the factory worker.

Who was the biggest single employer in America at the beginning of the '90s?

If you said General Motors, go to the foot of the class. It was McDonald's.

Who was second?

If you said Burger King, go to the head of the class. The federal government was third and Sears, Roebuck was fourth.

What has happened to the army of blue-collar workers who used to support their families comfortably on factory paychecks?

Computers and robots have taken their jobs. Willard A. Daggett, director of occupational education instruction for the state of New York, gave a dramatic account of the way automation affected QR Industries, a company that produces steel products, including steel clamps that go on hoses in General Motors cars:

> In 1985, QR Industries had 300 people making these clamps. In 1989, however, our sons and daughters would have a difficult time going to work for QR Industries. Today, they make the steel clamps, put them into a box, and put a bar code on the box. The label can be read by an optical scanner—just like ones seen in supermarkets. The box goes into a truck for shipping.
>
> In the middle of the truck is a conveyor belt. One of the things on that bar code is information stating the 20-minute window during which the box must arrive on the General Motors loading dock. The bar code is read by an optical character reader and communicated to a little computerized monitor on the dashboard of the truck that says when it's to be delivered and where. If it arrives 10 minutes early, there's a penalty. If it arrives 10 minutes late, there's a penalty.
>
> When the truck arrives within its 20-minute window, a robot-like machine comes off the loading dock, enters the truck, reads the bar codes, pulls off the correct boxes, takes them into General Motors and sets them on the assembly line. Another robot-like machine opens the boxes, and a third one leans over and picks up the clamps. If a clamp is

1/100 of an inch off, QR Industries is penalized 70 clamps. That's their contract. Why? Because the robot can't pick it up if it's more than 1/100 of an inch off.

What happens if they reject one in 100 clamps? How many do QR Industries get paid for? Thirty, because they're penalized 70. Suppose it rejects two. You would not want to be the owner of QR Industries, would you? In 1986, when the new contract was written, it was rejecting five clamps in every 100, so QR Industries had to become more precise. They had to do better work. So they introduced all types of short-term training programs. After continued failure, they made a major change in their system. QR Industries did exactly what General Motors had done. It robotized its assembly line. Now one clamp in 10,000 is rejected.[1]

What did this mean in human terms?

The number of people on the QR assembly line dropped from 300 to 17. The accounts receivable clerk, who filled out the bill and recorded the data for QR, was replaced by a bar code that reported directly to the computer system via the optical scanner. The bar code also replaced the receiving clerk and accounting clerk at General Motors. QR Industries has a contract stating that within 24 hours of the receipt of its clamps, an electronic bank transfer must be made into its bank account. It's done by computer. So who needs a bunch of people sitting at desks in an accounting department?

These changes have a profound bearing on the future prospects of millions of Americans. The high-school graduate can no longer go down to the employment office at the local factory and sign on for a job that will offer comfortable wages and a good benefits

---

[1] Willard A. Daggett, "Future Workplace Is Shocking," *North Carolina Education,* November/December 1990, p. 4.

package. For those who fail to prepare themselves for the age of computers and robots, the prospects lean toward minimum-wage jobs flipping burgers and checking groceries.

## MISS THELMA TRANSFERS DOWNWARD

These changes don't just affect assembly-line workers and machine operators. They affect us all. As I speak to various groups about the challenges of the future, I like to tell the story of Miss Thelma, the Tar Heel school teacher who died after spending 40 years in the classroom. When the school bells rang inside the Pearly Gates, she was there, faithful school marm that she was.

Saint Peter proudly showed her to a beautiful modern classroom, high-tech beyond your imagination. There was a computer screen at every desk, and those jewels didn't just blink at you; they talked.

Miss Thelma looked around the room at the bright-faced young cherubs who had just taken their seats, their halos gleaming, their wings neatly folded.

"This is all very nice," said Miss Thelma to Saint Peter. "But I just can't handle it. I never had anything like this back in North Carolina. I don't know a thing about computers, and I don't feel comfortable in this room."

"I'm sorry," said Saint Peter regretfully, "but this is all we have."

Miss Thelma glanced around the room once more, then asked: "Can I get a transfer?"

One call did it, and Miss Thelma was sent down to the other school district. She was ushered into another classroom—the kind she had taught in for 40 years. It had the four walls, the alphabet over the blackboard, the flag at a 45-degree angle, and the pictures of the presidents—George Washington on the right, and Abraham Lincoln on the left. It was steamy hot in there, naturally, but Miss Thelma was used to the heat of a Carolina summer, so she didn't mind. The desks were in nice little rows, and Miss Thelma looked into the faces of all the little imps who had pestered her for 40 years. She smiled pleasantly as she had done for 40 years, and the imps grinned wickedly, as they had done for 40 years. Miss Thelma was back in the same old rut.

The moral to the story is this: "You can change or you can go to hell."

# A CENTURY OF RAPID CHANGE

We've seen a lot of technological change already in the 20th century. In fact, change has been the one constant in these turbulent times. Look at some of the progress we've seen:

The first airplane flew in 1904. By 1969 we had put men on the moon.

In 1901, the German ship *Deutschland* crossed the Atlantic in five days, 11 hours and five minutes—the fastest crossing up to that time. In 1978, a Concorde passenger jet flew from Paris to New York in three hours, 30 minutes and 11 seconds, but that was a yawner. Prior to that, Soviet Cosmonaut Yuri Gagarin had circled the earth in one hour and 48 minutes. And in 1969, American astronauts reached the moon in little more than half the time it took the *Deutschland* to cross the Atlantic.

My parents have never flown. For their generation, an airplane flight was something only the most daring would undertake. I have flown jetliners at 500 miles per hour or better, at distances of six to seven miles above the earth. Within my life span, I expect that I will have the option of traveling by suborbital space plane from North America to Asia in less time than it takes my parents to go from Tabor City to Myrtle Beach.

In 1900 there were no aspirins, no penicillin, no EKGs. Open-heart surgery was unthinkable. Organ transplants were the stuff of science fiction. Pneumonia was a dreaded disease, because it was often fatal. Even within my memory, polio was a scourge. Families used to keep track of the latest polio epidemic through newspaper headlines the way we now keep track of the paths of hurricanes. Who knows what medical vistas will be opened to us through gene-splicing and other advanced biochemical techniques of the 21st century?

When I was young, people still drove Model A's for everyday transportation. Automatic transmissions were novelties, and only the most shameless show-off would buy a car with air conditioning. In rural areas, the outdoor privy was the rule rather than the exception. Air conditioning consisted of an open window, a fan and a glass of ice water.

We have gone from primitive wireless sets to color televisions receiving signals bounced off satellites or fed from VCRs sitting atop our receivers. We have gone from fixed-focus Kodak cameras to automatic-focus camcorders and still cameras that set focus and exposure by computers. The computer has transformed our lives in ways many of us still can't imagine. And we haven't seen the end of it.

# SOCIOLOGICAL CHANGE

Technological change has been matched by sociological change. Attitudes toward love and marriage have undergone drastic revision. Women as well as men are expected to sow their wild oats before marriage, and for many, marriage is just one of several lifestyle options.

The shape and texture of the American work force has changed dramatically. So has the structure of the American family.

These changes have taken place in large measure since I entered high school. During the '50s decade, the typical American household included the breadwinner father, the homemaker mother (who, of course, was married to the father), and two children of public-school age.

Today, only fewer than 5% of American households fit that model. That means that more than 95% of American households fall into one or more of these categories:

** Both parents work outside the home.

** The head of the household is a single parent.

** The family includes stepchildren.

** The family consists of a childless couple.

The prospects for a return to the traditional family seem slim at present. More than one-third of all the marriages performed are second marriages for at least one partner. More and more celebrities—role models for many among the emerging generation—are choosing to bear "love children" unfettered by the bonds of matrimony.

Remember the hue and cry Hollywood raised when Ingrid Bergman became pregnant by a man who was not her husband? Remember when school teachers weren't expected to date, much less have babies?

We've come a long way. I remember the time when I was school psychologist in Summerville, South Carolina, and a new teacher was facing a conference with the mother of a problem child. The teacher was about five months pregnant, and her small stature seemed to exaggerate the condition. The mother of the problem child was quite a large lady. She wore a floral dress with a scarf tied tight around her neck, and she presented an imposing figure. Intimidating, even.

The mother looked down at the little pregnant teacher and said: "Huh! You Leon's teacher, right? Leon told me you'd been messin' around."

The teacher, as it happened, was married, but in an age not far removed from memory, she would have been out of job, marriage license or not.

We will see some sociological changes as the American population ages. The Baby Boomers will be applying for senior citizenship in the early years of the 21st century. By the turn of the century, octogenarians will outnumber teen-agers. There will be a tremendous reservoir of knowledge and experience among the older generation. This will present us with opportunities as well as problems.

# CHANGES IN THE WORK PLACE

In the work place, we've already seen dramatic change. If you were to look across a factory floor 40 years ago, chances are you would have seen a predominance of white male workers, except in those few low-wage industries that were traditional employers of women. If you looked behind executive desks, you would almost certainly be looking at white males, mostly of Anglo-Saxon or other northern European stock.

Today, white males make up fewer than half the members of the American work force. By the turn of the century, only one in eight workers will be white male. These changes are being brought about by a number of factors. Sociological change is one of them. Women and minorities are demanding equal justice in the work place. Demographic change is another. The birth rate among minorities is higher than it is among Caucasians. Finally, immigration, which has energized American society for so much of its history, continues apace. But the newcomers, in the main, are not Europeans. They're coming from Latin America and from Asia. Those who have arrived before them have struggled for an environment in which females and non-WASPs no longer have to play bit roles in the American work place.

# THE BABY BOOM GOES BUST

Another factor affecting the work environment of the early 21st century is the labor crunch. Humans are a renewable resource, but it takes a generation or two to renew it. The Baby Boomer generation was their parents' way of renewing human resources that had been exhausted by low birth rates during the Depression and World War II. The boom lasted from 1946 through 1964. Starting in the early '70s, these boomers entered adulthood, began seeking jobs and started setting up households. They became producers and consumers, spurring the nation's lusty post-war economic growth. There has been no comparable reproductive upsurge since. In fact, small families have become part of the desirable "lifestyle" of the late 20th century. A small crop of babies today means a small crop of workers 20 years down the road.

"Things will be dramatically different," said John Rees, an economic geographer and professor at the University of North Carolina at Greensboro. "We're talking about a sea change, not just a watershed."[2]

We are now dealing with the conditions spawned by a series of short crops of babies.

The adult population of Americans has grown by more than 2% a year since the early '70s. During the early '90s, the rate sank to 1%, and is expected to drop further. The number of new households is shrinking. During the '70s, about 1.6 million new ones were started each year. During 1990, the number was just over half a million. It is not inconceivable that the number of households in the country will actually shrink.

The crunch began to make itself felt toward the end of the '80s. By this time, we were well into the post-industrial age with a consequent emphasis on knowledge and high technology. This created a great need for highly literate people. But the need arose just when American schools were turning out a short crop of fully literate graduates.

The competition for college graduates began heating up, and the trend will continue through the '90s and beyond. That means

---

[2] Tom Edmonds, "From Boom to Bust," *Triad Business*, Greensboro, North Carolina, March 11–18, 1991, Vol. 5, No. 47, p.1

that fully literate, highly competent workers will be at a premium in the 21st century. You can begin preparing yourself now to exploit this seller's market in knowledge and skills.

# THE CHANGING CORPORATION

Who will be the winners in tomorrow's career competition?

The people who are prepared to meet the changing needs of corporate organizations.

The 21st century will offer an entirely different type of corporation from the kind that ushered in the 20th century.

In 1900, a corporation was looked upon as a machine. Every component had a function, which it was expected to fulfill regardless of how the other components functioned. Accounting did its job, regardless of how well the Sales Department was functioning. Engineering took care of its duties and let Production look out for itself. Each of these departments had a head, who reported to someone higher up the corporate chart until the rarefied atmosphere of the executive suite was reached. It was a strictly hierarchical arrangement. The production worker talked to the line supervisor, who talked to the superintendent, who talked to the department head, who talked to the divisional manager, who talked to the vice president, who talked to the president, who talked to the CEO, who talked to God.

Production workers didn't have to think. All they had to do was receive and execute orders. The CEO didn't have to worry about what production workers thought. They were just so many interchangeable parts. Corporations were run on much the same principle as Vince Lombardi ran his football teams. As one writer put it:

> "For Lombardi, a team was not eleven individuals, some
> of them more dependable than others. It was one unit with
> 11 parts, and when one part ceased to function, the whole
> unit broke down; the chances of that breakdown were reduced

when the responsibilities of each player were kept simple but interconnected."[3]

That system worked in the corporate world so long as workers were willing to function in the role of robots in exchange for livable wages. But as the 20th century delivered more affluence and more leisure, the work force gained an awareness of other values besides a regular paycheck. Quality of life became important too.

In addition, the emergence of the global marketplace forced American companies to pursue an unprecedented level of excellence in order to remain competitive. This level of excellence could not be achieved by human robots trained to work without thinking.

## ORGANISMS, NOT MACHINES

Corporate thinking has taken a new direction as we near the edge of the 21st century. Corporations are no longer perceived as machines, but as living, evolving organisms in which each component has a stake in the well-being of the whole. In an automobile, the starter may lead a separate existence from the steering wheel, though the car needs both to function. But in a living body, the welfare of one part is directly tied in with the welfare of the whole. When your stomach is upset, you're miserable all over. When the hammer hits your thumb, your head knows it immediately.

We have learned, therefore, that for quality and excellence to be reflected in a corporate product, they must permeate the organization. That means that the production worker, no less than the CEO, has to be thinking quality. The new attitude is epitomized in the advertising slogan of Ford Motor Company: "Quality is Job 1."

---

[3] Tom Dowling, *Coach: A Season with Lombardi* (New York: Popular Library, by arrangement with W. W. Norton & Company, Inc.), p. 85.

# GOOD-BYE TO THE HIERARCHY

How has Ford pursued this objective?

For one thing, by dismantling the hierarchical system that had prevailed since Henry Ford founded the company and sent it down the assembly line to greatness.

When Don Petersen rose to corporate power with Ford, he declared war on what he called "chimneys of power." He required engineers to talk to production people, designers to talk to sales people, and people of all levels to talk to production workers.

The policy bore fruit in the design and manufacture of the Taurus car of the '80s. Until that time, Ford's typical approach to producing a new model was to let each department take a separate whack at it.

The designers would come up with an overall design, then hand it to the engineers. The engineers would design the mechanical workings and pass it on to manufacturing. Manufacturing would figure out how to make it, then turn it over to marketing. Marketing would come up with a marketing plan, then hand it to sales. Sales would go out and sell.

The Taurus was handled differently. Ford was awash in red ink and perilously close to hitting the slippery slope toward bankruptcy. The energy crunch had given the small-car manufacturers of Japan and Europe an edge on the American industry, which had acquired a reputation for producing gas-guzzling clunkers. This car had to be different.

Petersen, then the president of Ford, put Lewis Veraldi in charge of a team that cut across departmental lines. Early in the project, Veraldi obtained input from design, production, sales, marketing and others with a stake in the product.

Everybody from assembly-line workers to corporate executives was asked, "If you were building this car, how would you do it?"

# 1,000 FRESH IDEAS

The assembly-line workers alone offered 1,000 workable ideas. A member of the design team, for instance, approached two assembly-line workers in Atlanta who were juggling an instrument panel. In the past, designers didn't talk to production workers. But this one had a question:

"What can we do to make your job easier?

The production workers had a quick reply:

"Put in a small locater pin so we can put this panel in the same place every time."

It was a minor suggestion but it meant a boost in quality for the product—and in the ease of assembling it. And it came from people who knew what they were talking about.

Suggestions of this kind helped make the Taurus a huge success, and Ford came roaring back to profitability.

What happened?

Ford, in a sense, turned all its workers into entrepreneurs. It gave them a stake in the product. They responded in innovative ways.

# JUDGMENT DAY IS EVERY DAY

Successful corporate leaders of the 21st century will be those who are able to provide that kind of innovation and to elicit it from the people they lead. Companies can no longer afford to develop a tried and true product and stick with it until some distant Judgment Day. That's because Judgment Day is every day in the worldwide marketplace.

Remember the Model T? It kept the Ford Motor Company in business for a nearly a decade and a half. Henry Ford developed a tried and true product and stuck with it. It paid off for a while. But along came General Motors with the concept of planned obsolescence. The annual model change became the norm, and Ford's slowness to adapt to the changing market caused it to lose its pre-eminent place in the automotive world.

The change that overtook Ford in the '20s was glacial compared with the changes that corporations of the '90s are dealing with, and the scenario of the '90s is sure to be fast-forwarded during the 21st century.

To sustain this pace of change, the 21st century corporation will be leaner and flatter than its 20th century counterpart. Decision-making will be pushed farther down the corporate chart. The rewards will go not to those who can receive and execute orders from above but to those who can innovate and spread the innovative spirit throughout the organization.

In the work place of this decade and beyond, the successful boss is one who leads and inspires, not one who orders and intimidates.

# THE COMMUNICATIONS REVOLUTION

The work place of the 21st century will differ radically in another respect: It will not be geographically tied to a specific location. During the 20th century, the automobile, with the help of the freeways, cut populations loose from their inner-city moorings. The suburbs flourished and inner cities decayed.

During the 21st century, electronics and telecommunications will have a similar effect on a national scale. They will disperse people from metropolitan centers to less populated regions, as physical location becomes less and less relevant in a world of instant communication. It's already happening. When a secretary in Atlanta telephones for a hotel reservation in San Francisco, the person taking the reservation may be in Wichita. Few settlements in this country are beyond the reach of fax machines, and the ubiquitous telephone line can grant quick access to computerized data banks a continent away. A sales manager no longer has to fly salespeople to a central location for a conference. Electronic communications enables them to confer while sitting at desks scattered from Waterville, Maine, to El Centro, California; from Yakima, Washington, to Homestead, Florida.

So look for many smaller and medium-sized businesses to relocate in the rural areas that once were too remote for them to consider. And look for corporations of the future to fill their brainpower positions with people who can do their jobs by modem and fax machine while enjoying the advantages of rural living in places such as Tabor City, North Carolina.

## SHRINKING GLOBE, MUSHROOMING MARKETS

As advanced communications shrink the nation, they will also shrink the world. We are already well into the transition to a global economy. The American market is no longer the preserve of General Motors, Ford and Chrysler; of Westinghouse, General Electric and Motorola; of IBM, Hewlett Packard and Xerox. American companies must not only defend their domestic turf against high-quality products from abroad; they must also take their products to foreign turf and sell them.

Just as individuals must achieve an awareness of opportunities beyond their immediate back yards, so corporations must achieve awareness of opportunities in the global market. We have been accustomed to functioning in a domestic market of about 200 million people. While we were developing that market, another market of 200 million people developed almost overnight across our back yard, on the opposite side of the Pacific Ocean.

Japan achieved the status of an economic superpower, with living standards comparable to those in Western Europe. Its population of 120 million is nearly as great as that of the United States at the outset of World War II. Japan is part of a dynamic regional economic sphere that includes Taiwan, South Korea, Hong Kong and Singapore.

*40*

The economic growth of Japan and these "little tigers" has produced a bumper crop of consumers waiting to be enticed by American products. They will become important sources for suppliers, investors and joint-venture partners.

The Chinese mainland is another potential market. Its sheer size—1.2 billion people—imbues it with potential. If the huge country ever gains political stability, it will offer enormous opportunities for American companies.

Eastern Europe has been a gold mine of potential waiting to be exploited by capitalist ingenuity. The communist system produced a well-educated population accustomed to low wages, but without the dynamism that springs from political freedom and an unfettered marketplace. Now Eastern Europe is turning to free-market socialism, and the opportunities are great.

Among the first American firms to exploit it has been Levi Strauss. For years, Eastern Europeans have been in love with American jeans, often offering to buy them off the bodies of Western tourists. Now Levi Strauss and other American companies have launched 1,000 joint ventures in Hungary alone, and more than 200 in Poland.

# GLOBAL OUTLOOK: WHERE IS JAKARTA?

This means that the people who succeed in the 21st century must acquire a global outlook. They must know the globe as thoroughly as the 20th century tycoon knew the United States.

Where is Jakarta? Did you know it is the capital of the fifth most populous country on earth? A country with 180 million people? If you don't know where Indonesia is, how big it is, and what its economic potential is, find out. You'll be hearing about it in the 21st century.

Where is Myanmar? Did you know that it is larger than France and is 80% as populous? We used to call it Burma, and it is one of the "sleeping tigers" of the Orient.

Where will you find the largest gross domestic product in the world? Not in the United States and not in Japan, but in the European Community, an organization of European states that integrated their economies into a common market.

What kind of opportunities will be available subsequent to the collapse of communism in Eastern Europe? The successful executives of the 21st century will be the ones who find out the quickest.

They will also be the ones who are best at studying and mastering the geographical, cultural, economic and social facts about other nations and peoples.

## CHOCOLATE AND CULTURE

People from other countries know much more about us than we know about them. That gives them an advantage when it comes to selling their products here. The Japanese know what turns on the American consumer. We know little about what turns on the Oriental consumer.

An American who traveled on the Chinese mainland returned to tell about the milk-chocolate bars he had bought at a hotel counter. The milk chocolate, made in Shanghai, was of excellent quality—on a par with the milk chocolate available in this country. But the thing that struck him was the wrapper. It wasn't the plain chocolate-brown wrapper with the brand name in block letters that so readily identifies the Hershey Bar in America. Each wrapper bore a beautiful color picture of a different Chinese landscape.

Later, the American spoke with an official from Taiwan, who explained why the mainlanders invested in the decorative wrappers.

In America, he said, candy bars are items bought, frequently on impulse, by casual customers. We buy them for our kids, or we buy them for a quick energy fix. A distinctive wrapper with the brand name prominently displayed is an advantage in our market, because when we want a chocolate bar, we don't just want *any* chocolate bar. We usually have our favorites.

In the Orient, candy bars are not bought that way, the Taiwanese official explained. Oriental parents don't indulge their children with chocolate on demand, and Oriental children don't go around with money burning holes in their pockets. Candy is usually bought by adults to be passed around to adult guests. It's considered a gracious gesture, and the host's prestige rides not only on the taste of the chocolate but also on the impressiveness of the wrapper. Beautiful wrappers, such as those on the Shanghai chocolates, impress the guests and enhance the standing of the host.

Therefore, a Hershey Bar in its chocolate-colored wrapper doesn't stand a ghost of a chance against a chocolate bar from the Orient wrapped in festive foil. The Japanese and Taiwanese understand these cultural nuances. Do we?

The Japanese, Taiwanese, South Koreans and Singaporeans also know about American customs, American culture and American history.

On the banquet circuit, I like to tell the story of the little Japanese girl in the Horry County School System. We'll call her Tapioka. She was easily the brightest kid in the class, a fact that irritated Johnny Matthews, whose scholastic prowess she had eclipsed.

One day the teacher was asking some questions on American history.

"Who said, 'Give me liberty or give me death'?" asked the teacher.

Tapioka's hand shot up first.

"Patrick Henry, 1775!" she replied.

"Who said, 'I only regret that I have but one life to lose for my country'?" asked the teacher.

Tapioka's hand went up again.

"Nathan Hale, 1776!" she answered.

"Who said 'Ask not what your country can do for you; ask what you can do for your country'?"

"John F. Kennedy, 1961!" said Tapioka.

"Damn the Japanese," blurted Johnny Matthews, unable to contain his resentment any longer.

"Lee Iacocca, 1985!" responded Tapioka.

## NO DECOLLETAGE IN ARABIA

As our troops in Saudi Arabia learned, often to their chagrin, Moslem culture also has a different set of values from ours. An American company once sent a team of men and women executives to Saudi Arabia. A woman executive showed up in a low-cut diaphanous dress that would have been smashing at a Manhattan cocktail party but proved offensive to the conservative Moslem culture her company was trying to penetrate. The host company did not invite her to subsequent occasions.

Such pitfalls abound on the international business scene, and Americans must learn to avoid them if they expect to hold their own in global competition.

## LEARN THE LANGUAGE

Someone once said that Japan has 10,000 salespeople in New York City, and every one of them speaks English. The United States has 10,000 salespeople in all of Japan, and every one of them speaks English.

Americans are notoriously tongue-tied when it comes to speaking to foreigners. We have been spoiled by the fact that our native tongue has become the *lingua franca*—the common language—of international commerce. Nearly a billion people speak English, and it is the official or semi-official language of 60 countries. But people from other countries take pride in their languages too.

If you're trying to persuade Mademoiselle de la Salle, Signora Lombardi, Herr Schmidt or Lao Chen to do business with your company, you'll have a head start if you can at least say "Hello,"

"Thank You" and "Goodbye" in the language of your prospective partner. You'll be even farther ahead if you can say in the foreign tongue, "I'm sure that we can arrange a loan through the Export-Import Bank and we will establish a service branch in your city to take care of any problems after the sale." A vocabulary of 500 to 1,000 words is not hard to acquire, and it can take you a long way in any language.

## OTHER TIPS ON SUCCESS

Here are some other tips for success in the 21st century:

** Learn to vision. Corporate leaders of the future must learn to create visions and communicate them to every level of the company. A vision tells the people what kind of company they're working for, what its goals are and how it expects to achieve them. The vision provides the dynamic nucleus around which a company is organized.

** Learn to speak in public. The successful executives of the future will not be autocrats who issue decrees from the boardroom; they'll be leaders who can inspire team-work within the corporation and confidence among customers, clients and stockholders. Lee Iacocca's ability as a communicator surely has been a major factor in the resurrection of the Chrysler Corporation.

** Learn to write effectively. Company visions and policies must be transmitted through the written as well as the spoken word. Think of the power exerted by such documents as Magna Carta, the Declaration of Independence, and Woodrow Wilson's 14 Points. An eloquent written statement of the company's philosophy and mission can be a powerful motivator and guide to prosperity.

*45*

** Develop an interest in the arts. The arts are well on their way to surpassing sports as the nation's top leisure-time interest. During the past two decades, museum attendance increased from 200 million to 500 million and opera audiences tripled. In 1988, Americans spent $3.7 billion on the arts and $2.8 billion on sports events. Sponsorship of artistic events has become a popular and profitable venture of successful businesses. Business people have found that a knowledge of the arts is helpful in building rapport with decision-makers and, therefore, in obtaining their business.

** Stay attuned to the environment. As author Patricia Aburdene noted in a magazine article:

> The end of the cold war and the reversal of the arms race have freed humanity to deal with the next gigantic problem on its agenda—the global environment. Environmental concerns will reverberate throughout the 1990s because the issue affords individuals daily opportunities to take a stand. . . . No CEO who aims to keep the company in the green can afford to disparage environmental issues in the 1990s. The environmental trend will command center stage in multibillion-dollar consumer industries. Companies that use animals for testing will uncover new product tests or face a greater outcry from the animal-rights lobby. Less packaging and more recycled packaging will be primary concerns in the U.S. food industry, among others.[4]

** Learn as much as you can about the different ways in which people think, respond and are motivated. This knowledge can be extremely helpful as you work in

---

[4] Patricia Aburdene, "How to Think Like a CEO for the '90s," *Working Woman,* September 1990, pp. 134–137.

the teamwork atmosphere that will pervade the 21st century work place.

# DON'T FIGHT THE LAST WAR

There's a saying that generals are always fighting the last war. Those who do are those who lose. The French lost the opening stage of World War II by putting their faith in the Maginot Line, a system of fortifications that had been effective in stopping armies of the past. The Poles tried to stop Hitler's modern armor with mounted cavalry. The Iraqis believed that the factors that worked in favor of the North Vietnamese against the United States during the '60s and '70s would work in their favor in the '90s.

The generals who planned Desert Storm decided not to fight the last war. They used futuristic weapons and tactics and administered a devastating defeat to Iraq.

Let us hope that the competition of the 21st century will be more peaceful. But you will not prosper in the next century by following the strategies of this century.

You will not achieve success in agriculture by plowing a straight furrow behind a mule. You will not achieve success in the corporate world by learning to give and take orders. You will not survive in an era of innovation by sticking with the tried and true. You will not win in global competition by focusing your attention on the folks in Peoria.

# THE PAST IS PROLOGUE; THE DRAMA'S IN THE FUTURE

"The past is prologue," wrote Shakespeare in "The Tempest." In a play, a prologue is an introductory statement that precedes the actual drama. We can use the immediate past as an introduction to the future, but we can't use it as a blueprint. The future has a shape and form of its own. We ought to study the past for any insights it might offer on the drama yet to come. But our chief concern should be with the future, for, as Charles F. Kettering observed, "we will have to spend the rest of our lives there."

# Chapter Three

# *There Are No Self-made People*

*No man is an island entire of itself; every man is a piece of the continent, a part of the main. . . .*

*—JOHN DONNE*

We have to be receptive to the assistance of others. Somehow, we have to draw them to us, welcome their attention and demonstrate to them that their efforts in our behalf are not fruitless. By opening ourselves to this assistance from others, we accumulate teachers, mentors and benefactors who give us the needed push at critical times. Such generous people have ways of knowing the difference between highly motivated people who need only a boost toward self-sufficiency and sluggards who are simply waiting around for a free ride.

# WE ALL NEED HELP

The next time you hear someone say, "There goes a self-made woman," or "There goes a self-made man," file the statement away with these other fallacies:

** The Earth is flat.

** Japanese products are cheap and shoddy.

** You don't need to floss to have healthy teeth and gums.

Believe that flossing is unnecessary, and you may end up putting your teeth in a jar overnight.

Buy the doctrine that Japanese products are cheap and shoddy, and you may end up choosing between the unemployment line and the job-application line at the nearest Honda plant.

Insist on believing that the Earth is flat, and you will fall off the success wagon as soon as you reach the edge of your narrow horizon.

Believe you can become a self-made success, and you should prepare yourself for lonely failure.

God is the only entity I know of who is capable of success on his own, and even he chose to create a universe of companions.

When Justice Oliver Wendell Holmes Jr. turned 90, a reporter asked him the secret of his success. His reply: "Young man, the secret of my success is that at an early age I discovered I was not God."

Those of us who are not God need all the help we can get. I got it and I welcomed it. The givers of that help left footprints on my heart. I only hope that I have returned the favor and can continue to do so.

# PARENTAL FOOTPRINTS

The first people to leave footprints on my heart were my parents. They were—and are—hard-working, honest, and clean-living.

Though I sometimes chafed at their Puritanical lifestyle, I now know that many of the things I resented have helped build in me the strength I needed to succeed.

When I was growing up, I thought my dad and mom were crazy. I was embarrassed to have friends come to my house, because we never had coffee or tea or cola. If we wanted something to drink, we had milk. Not the pasteurized, homogenized stuff that came from the dairy in Wilmington, but the straight stuff from our own cows. We had water. Not the aerated, chlorinated, fluorinated, stuff that comes from the local filtration plant, but clean pure water straight from the ground. We had lemonade. The lemonade Dad made in the summertime must have been what God had in mind when he created the lemon. Every now and then we could get little bottles of grape drink—"penny drink" we called it. That was about the most exotic beverage you'd find at our house. But my grandmother kept Pepsi in her refrigerator, and I loved to go to her house and let the forbidden bubbly cola slide down my throat.

Alcohol and tobacco were strictly taboo. We lived in the Carolina Tobacco Belt, but my dad's conscience told him to stop growing the weed, even though it was the most profitable crop he could have grown. His conscience was telling him that tobacco was harmful long before the surgeon-general got on the bandwagon.

I didn't realize it then, but my parents were giving me a foundation of good nutrition and good health habits that were to keep me well supplied with vital energy as I fought for success.

Dad was even ahead of the health experts when it came to the harmful effects of the sun. While all the other kids came home from the Grand Strand sporting beautiful tans, Dad insisted that we remain pale. We had to keep our heads covered in the sun, and he insisted that we wear long sleeves. I fought that, but now research has shown that overexposure to the sun is a leading cause of skin cancer. My dad was right.

# GENEROSITY AND HARD WORK

My parents inculcated other values in me too. They were Good Samaritans of the first order. If someone's house caught fire, they always took the family something to replace their lost things. If there was ever a stranger around who needed a meal, they provided the meal. I never knew who was going to be at the dinner table. That Good Samaritan tradition became a part of my life and I cherish it today.

They also taught me not to be afraid of hard work. That lesson was invaluable as I began working to help pay my way through college and, later, to advance my career. Farming in those days was a family venture, and everyone was expected to work. I was the water girl for the older family members before I was old enough to take part in the more strenuous work.

Later, I joined in the planting and hoeing and harvesting, and I did more than my fair share. I would work with Dad and the boys during the morning hours, then go home and help Mama fix lunch. While the boys were lolling on the floor, I was working over a hot stove and, later, helping clear the table and wash dishes. Then I'd pick up my hoe and trudge back to the fields with them. Women's liberation had not reached the farm back then, and the menfolk seemed to think it only natural that I pull double-duty as a field hand and house worker. But I felt discriminated against, and this resentment, in part, fueled my ambition toward a higher calling.

# A NURTURING BROTHER

My brothers, of course, were not being deliberately callous. They were conforming to the prevailing culture of the time. My older brother Harold, in fact, was a nurturing individual. It was he who took me under his wing that first day of school. It was Harold, too, who made it possible for me to have one of the richest cultural experiences of my public-school life. He took me on a field trip to Raleigh to see Sonja Henie skate. Just going to Raleigh, the state capital 100 miles from Tabor City, was exciting enough. But Sonja Henie's performance was an event from another world.

# EDUCATIONAL FOOTPRINTS

My parents' attitude toward higher education ranged somewhere between indifference and hostility, but I am not resentful. They left good and lasting footprints on my heart in other areas of life. Others would provide the educational footprints.

Anne Brooks McGougan was the first, of course. That dear teacher was not playing favorites. She approached all her pupils with that same loving attention to individual needs. Why, then, did her footsteps leave permanent imprints on my heart while on other hearts they faded like my footprints in the farm soil?

The answer is that we have to be receptive to the assistance of others. Somehow, we have to draw them to us, welcome their attention and demonstrate to them that their efforts in our behalf are not fruitless.

By opening ourselves to this assistance from others, we accumulate teachers, mentors and benefactors who give us the needed push at critical times. Such generous people have ways of knowing the difference between highly motivated people who need only a boost toward self-sufficiency and sluggards who are simply waiting around for a free ride.

President Ronald Reagan used to say that there are two ways of dealing with a hungry man. One is to give him a fish, in which case he will be hungry again tomorrow. The other is to teach him to fish, in which case he will be able to feed himself in the future.

My benefactors sensed in me an eagerness to learn to fish, and they showed me how.

What was it that made Miss McGougan kneel beside me and offer me that all-important reassurance on the first day of school when I had flunked the Humpty Dumpty test?

Something in my demeanor told her what was in my heart: I
knew I was ignorant, but I wanted desperately to learn.

Miss McGougan put me to the test and I responded enthusiasti-
cally. I was like a little bird with my mouth open—eager for knowledge and for the approval of my teachers. By the end of that first
year, Miss McGougan knew that this girl was not out for a free
ride.

# HOME VALUES VERSUS SCHOOL HONORS

As I made my way up through the grades, I thrived on success.
I had to be self-motivated, because my achievements were often
doused in cold water when I brought them home. It wasn't that my
parents were uncaring; it's just that they subscribed to a set of values
that was at odds with many of the activities at school.

I remember the time when I was in second grade and won the
coloring contest for grades one through four. The subject was Cinder-
ella, and I did a beautiful job, meticulously coloring within the
lines. The prize was a certificate entitling me to a year of free movies
at the theater uptown.

I came home all excited over the honor. I showed my certificate
to my parents. But I had lost sight of my dad's attitude toward
movies. They were, in his mind, the work of the devil.

"There will be no picture shows around here," he told me.
And he threw my certificate in the fireplace. I can still see it going
up in flames. And I can still feel the pain over being denied something
I felt I had deserved.

I also remember the time David Earl Fipps and I were named
Valentine's king and queen for the fourth grade. We were to receive
our crowns at an evening ceremony at the VFW hut, just down the
street from the school. It was a social affair involving grades 1
through 7. My older brothers brought me to town for the big event.
Then word reached Dad that Muriel had gone into town for some
kind of party.

Dad came to the VFW hut in his pick-up truck and took me home before the ceremony took place. I never received my crown.

## A MOTIVATING TEACHER

I was fortunate, though, to have others who encouraged me to develop my scholastic and social abilities.

Among them was Beth Woody, my high-school English teacher. It was she who got me involved with the school annual. It was she who steered me toward opportunities to achieve. I remember, in particular, the time she encouraged me to enter the Voice of Democracy speaking contest. I was self-conscious and embarrassed to speak before an audience. She would give me a short story from Reader's Digest to read before the class.

The practice paid off. I was competing against the brightest and wealthiest kids in town, including my friend, Anne Mallard (now Anne Mallard Sanders), daughter of the lawyer. And I won. I not only won the contest for the school, but I also went on to win against contestants from the whole county. Later, the Jaycees asked me to deliver my speech at their Christmas social event. This time, Dad didn't stop me. I was intoxicated with the thrill of learning and achieving. That Voice of Democracy plaque still hangs on my wall. So add Beth Woody to the list of people who left footprints on my heart.

## A PRINCIPAL WHO SHELLED BUTTERBEANS

There's one other person who deserves special mention. His name is Charlie Pinner. He was my high-school principal and the man who literally put me on the road to an education. It was he who drove me to Red Springs, North Carolina, to Flora Macdonald

College (now Saint Andrews Presbyterian College at Laurinburg, North Carolina), to enroll me as a student.

Charlie Pinner was a special kind of person. He spent 38 years as principal in Tabor City when he could have gone higher. He had entered the Army in 1918, and remained in Europe long enough after World War I to study for a quarter at the University of Paris. He had returned to the United States and obtained a degree. He quickly became superintendent of schools in Wake Forest, North Carolina. He served as a superintendent in North Carolina schools during the Depression, but grew weary and frustrated trying to run school systems with paltry funding. When he came to Tabor City as principal, he vowed never again to be a school superintendent.

Charlie Pinner was not the kind of principal who came to work at 8 in the morning and was gone by 4 P.M. He reached out and touched the community, and especially the young people who were entrusted to his care.

I remember the day he paid a house call on the Ward family. We were in the back yard under the pecan tree, shelling butterbeans. Mr. Pinner asked Mama to bring him a chair and a pan, and he sat there and shelled butterbeans with us. Shelling butterbeans was a semi-social event anyway. You talked while you shelled, and when he went away Mr. Pinner was better acquainted with the Wards and their children.

I obviously drew his attention as I progressed through school. Mr. Pinner knew what an education could do for me, and he helped me get it.

# $100 AND AN INTRODUCTION

I was able to obtain a $1,000 student loan, but he knew that was just the beginning. While in the Wake Forest area, he had become good friends with a Presbyterian minister, and they worked at a mission together. That Presbyterian minister, Dr. Marshall Scott

Woodson, went on to become president of Flora Macdonald College.

I didn't know at the time of Mr. Pinner's personal friendship with Dr. Woodson. All I knew was that my principal offered to drive me to Red Springs for an interview with the president of the college.

We made the two-hour drive on a Saturday. Mr. Pinner introduced me to Dr. Woodson.

"Tabor City High School has provided Muriel with a good foundation," he said. "But she's going to need a lot more. I think she's ready for an experience beyond high school, and I'm hoping you'll provide it for her."

There was no entrance exam; no SAT. But there was one other thing. Mr. Pinner reached into his wallet, pulled out a $100 bill, and handed it to Dr. Woodson.

"This is the beginning," he said. "She'll need some more financial assistance later on, but this is my commitment."

And so Muriel Ward, who had entered first grade in Tabor City not knowing who Humpty Dumpty was, now had a down payment on her college education.

Some may look at her today, consider her humble beginnings on a North Carolina dirt farm, and say, "There goes a self-made woman."

But I know better. So does Charlie Pinner. So does Beth Woody. So does Anne McGougan. So does my brother Harold. So do my parents. So do many others who, through the years, have given me a jump start just when I needed it.

# JUMP-STARTING A GENIUS

To pretend that you don't need to be jump-started occasionally is to indulge in supreme arrogance. You don't have to be poor or dumb or confused to need a boost. I've seen service trucks hooking jumper cables to Cadillacs, Lincolns, Mercedeses and BMWs. Those cars ran fine once they were started. They were just temporarily down in their batteries.

I remember a young man in one of my fourth-grade classes to whom I was able to give a boost when everyone else thought he needed someone to bring him down a notch or two. I'll call him Ben.

Ben had a reputation for brilliance. He also had a reputation for being a pain.

"You've got to watch him," warned one of his previous teachers. "He thinks he knows everything better than you do, and he'll try to take over your class."

I made up my mind that I was going to make friends with this young man. On the first day of school, Ben was easy to spot. He was the kid in the French beret riding the bicycle with the little satchel attached.

I smiled to myself. Yes, Ben *was* different.

When you teach school in the rural South, you expect to hear English spoken in a way that would make an Oxford scholar cringe and ask for a transfer to the Sudan. But Ben's English was letter-perfect. He was the epitome of an intellectual.

I decided to make Ben an ally instead of a rival.

"You know," I told him at the beginning of the term, "teaching fourth grade is a new experience for me. I've taught middle school and high school, and this is my first elementary experience. I'll really need your help with some of these reading classes."

Ben responded to the challenge. He took me on as a project and worked with me in teaching the other kids the things he grasped so quickly.

At the time, a fourth-grade teacher taught everything—including music and physical education. I knew that Ben had been trained in music, so I asked him to help me with the music class.

He looked over one of the songs in our song book.

"It's a little hard for fourth-graders to sing it in this arrangement," he said. So he rearranged it. And it worked out well.

Brilliant people such as Ben can go on to great things if they're challenged and encouraged. Or they can wallow in mediocrity if they're unchallenged or frustrated. Ben went on to great things. I'd like to think I gave him a timely boost, and that his heart bears the faint footprints of the woman who co-taught the fourth grade with him.

# THE CLAY CAN CHOOSE ITS SCULPTORS

We all start life as a lump of soft, pliable clay. That lump feels the sculpting hands of many individuals during its evolution into a mature individual. The evolution is never complete.

Unlike the lifeless clay, we can guide the evolution by responding to certain touches, resisting others. I chose as role models and mentors the people who offered me love and encouragement toward positive goals. I attracted them to me by demonstrating a thirst for knowledge, a willingness to work hard to acquire it, and an equal willingness to apply it toward constructive ends.

Your goals may lie in fields other than education. Whatever they are, look around for good people who can help you learn the things you need to learn. Cultivate them as friends and mentors. They will respond and will feel rewarded when you begin applying the lessons they've taught you. And when you need a jump-start toward success, they'll be there to provide it.

Don't be proud and refuse to accept help when it's offered just because you feel you could never repay your benefactor. You can repay the debt. You do it by giving someone else a boost when you've acquired the necessary knowledge, experience and where-withal.

# FIND USES FOR DEAD ELEPHANTS

And never look down your nose at any offer of help. A proud but poor student was working his way through college as a part-time reporter for the local newspaper. An old editor, knowing the lad often ran short of money for food a day or two before payday, offered to assign him to the civic club beat. The reporter covering civic clubs got his lunches free in return for writing articles about the luncheon speeches. The reporter hesitated about taking this offer, which he considered a close cousin to charity.

"Son," said the editor, "Whenever anybody offers you something free, go ahead and take it. Even if it's a dead elephant, take it. Somewhere you're going to find somebody who can use a dead elephant."

The reporter took the offer. He ate a lot of roast beef, chicken and peas, and he ate the same lunch every day, because all the civic clubs met at the same hotel, and the hotel did not vary its menu from one day to the next. But it filled the youth's stomach on days when he could afford nothing else. In addition to eating regularly, the student developed the art of writing lively stories about dull speeches. It served him well when he left college to pursue a career in journalism. He found a valuable piece of ivory in the dead elephant he had accepted.

# MAKING THE TEAM

Regardless of your circumstances in life or the assets you brought into this world, you succeed only to the extent that you function well within the framework of society. In the next century, in particular, the corporate world will set a premium on teamwork and on the ability to foster teamwork.

How do you achieve the ability to work with a team? By learning to rely on others and to inspire others to rely on you.

You don't achieve these skills in an isolation booth. You achieve them by interacting with others, opening yourself to the influence of others and, in turn, exerting your own efforts in behalf of others.

In the process, you will grow toward success. But you will not achieve success entirely on your own. There is no such thing as a self-made person. The world is full of caring, generous people who are eager to help you achieve everything you're capable of achieving. Let them help you.

# Chapter Four

## *Know Thyself*

*This above all: To thine own self be true, And it must follow, as the night the day, Thou canst not then be false to any man*

—*WILLIAM SHAKESPEARE*

To know yourself is to know how you respond to your environment and why. It is to know your strong points and how to exploit them. It is to know your weak points and how to strengthen them or compensate for them. Once you have taken inventory of yourself, you may be surprised at what a worthwhile person you are. You are unique among the world's five billion specimens, and that makes you special. But you share with all the other specimens the attributes that make them human, and that means you belong.

# THE PROPER STUDY OF MANKIND

The title for this chapter, "Know Thyself," is taken from an inscription at the Delphic Oracle. Alexander Pope, the 18th-century English poet, expanded on the thought:

> Know then thyself, presume not God to scan;
> The proper study of mankind is man.

While the precise nature of God may be beyond mortal ken, we have at the moment some five billion specimens of mankind to be studied *en masse* or individually. And each of us has at least one specimen whom we can study closely and intimately. It's the specimen we see reflected in the mirror. So let us follow the advice of the Delphic Oracle and of Alexander Pope: Know thyself. And let us heed the counsel that Shakespeare passed on through his character in Hamlet: "To thine own self be true."

To know yourself is to know how you respond to your environment and why. It is to know your strong points and how to exploit them. It is to know your weak points and how to strengthen them or compensate for them.

Once you have taken inventory of yourself, you may be surprised at what a worthwhile person you are. You are unique among the world's five billion specimens, and that makes you special. But you share with all the other specimens the attributes that make them human, and that means you belong.

# BUILD YOUR SELF-ESTEEM

Knowing yourself, then, can bring you self-esteem and self-confidence, and those qualities are necessary to success. All humans have within them the ingredients for success. The secret lies in discovering these ingredients and blending them into the proper formula.

Every human being is endowed by nature to achieve excellence in at least one area. Studies show that the top 20% of the people in every field of work never become unemployed. If you can find that area in which you naturally excel, then you'll be well on your way to success. Where is your field of excellence? The best place to look is in the areas that give you personal satisfaction. You can be excellent only in the things that you love to do. The key to your success may be right at your feet.

Too many people go through life as failures because they never take the time to look inside themselves for the ingredients of success.

I recently worked with a group of 100 seventh-graders who were considered "youths at risk."

I asked them to write down three things that they were good at. For most, it took a lot of help from some facilitators to help them come up with just one thing. The hardest question was this: "What is something you've done that you're proud of?"

All of us have, at one time or another, been proud of something we've done. It may have been a little thing, but we were proud of it.

We need to dig these little accomplishments out of our memories and keep bringing them to the fore. Otherwise, we may forget what worthwhile things we've done, and therefore what worthwhile people we are.

We should always be challenging ourselves. Only through these challenges can we learn how good we really are. Remember those students in Columbia who told me they couldn't read? They actually believed they couldn't. But a trip down the hall to the rest rooms convinced them that they could, indeed read. They learned something about themselves. And what they learned added to their self-esteem and better equipped them to succeed in life.

## CHOOSE QUALITY COMPANIONS

One good way to build your self-esteem is to associate with high-quality people. You're known by the company you keep, and if you keep poor company, the people who observe you will equate you with the poor company. If that is true of the perception of others, it's also true of your self-perceptions. If you see yourself in the company of third-rate people, you will think of yourself as third-rate too. In fact, when first-class people associate with second-class people, they all end up as third-class people. Early in life, I chose to associate myself with quality people—the Anne Mallards, the Beth Woodys, the Anne McGougans, the Charlie Pinners. By going along with first-class people, I rode first-class too.

# DON'T BE A PHONY

We all know people who try to be what they're not. We call them phonies. Nobody likes a phony. What's more, when you're a phony, you're subjecting yourself to unnecessary negative stress. You're constantly worried that someone will blow your cover by discovering the real you. You spend so much energy hiding the real you that you don't have enough left to carry the bogus you to success.

I was able to associate with quality people without being a phony. Why? Because I chose people whose values I respected and I made their values my values.

Rudyard Kipling maintained that if you want to be truly successful, you must be able to "talk with crowds and keep your virtue, or walk with kings—nor lose the common touch." The daughter of the North Carolina dirt farmer and well-driller remains proud of where she came from. But she never lost sight of where she wanted to go. And she cherishes the friends she made among the common crowd and in the corridors of power. In order to succeed, I've never had to pretend I was something I was not.

If you try to be someone or something you're not, you may find yourself struggling in a career or other pursuits for which you are not temperamentally suited. This can smother your chances for success.

How do you discover the real you?

First, by learning something about the larger group to which you belong: the human race.

# ALL ALIKE, EACH DIFFERENT

Although each of us is a unique individual, we each hold certain attributes in common with all other humans. And we share certain attributes with some humans but not with others.

Students of human behavior have developed exercises through which they can divide the entire human race into certain categories of behavior and temperament. While all of us have *some* of the attributes of each category, we each fall predominantly into one category or another.

Your basic temperament—your basic pattern of responding to the environment—remains stable over time. As David Keirsey and Marilyn Bates explain in their book, *Please Understand Me:*

> Of course, some change is possible, but it is a twisting
> and distortion of underlying form. Remove the fangs of a
> lion and behold a toothless lion, not a domestic cat.[5]

If you try to go fox hunting with a domestic cat, you will be disappointed. A cat is not equipped, by temperament or by physical endowment, to chase a fox, run it into the ground, and bay loudly to lead the hunter to the quarry. You let the cat catch mice and you let your hounds chase the fox.

If you were to try to plow with a dairy cow, you would be just as disappointed as you would be if you tried to milk a mule.

And you wouldn't enter a mule in the Kentucky Derby. Mule

---

[5] David Keirsey and Marilyn Bates, *Please Understand Me*, (Del Mar, California: Gnosology Books Ltd., 1984, distributed by Prometheus Nemesis Book Company) p. 2.

races are for comedy, not for serious sport. The mule lacks the competitive spirit of the Thoroughbred race horse. When one mule gets ahead of the other, it's likely to stop and wait for the other to catch up. It's in the nature of the mule, and generations of farmers have learned the futility of trying to change a mulish nature.

So what does that say for you as a human individual?

It means that you shouldn't try to succeed in endeavors for which you are not temperamentally suited. You will succeed by identifying your own temperament or behavior style and seeking fulfillment in pursuits that make use of its strong points.

# HIPPOCRATES AND 'HUMORS'

About 25 centuries ago, Hippocrates, the Greek "father of medicine," suggested that human behavior was governed by four "humors" or body fluids that controlled the way we responded. He identified these as choler (yellow bile), phlegm, melancholer (black bile) and blood (sanguis, in Latin). Thus, irritable people were described as choleric, dull and sluggish people as phlegmatic, gloomy and depressed people as melancholic, and bright, optimistic people as sanguine.

By the middle of the 20th century, behavioral scientists concluded that Hippocrates was on to something. Although they discounted the influence of the body humors, they did conclude that human temperament can be divided roughly into four different behavior styles.

# FOUR BASIC TEMPERAMENTS

During the '50s, Isabel Myers and her mother, Katheryn Briggs, developed 16 different categories of response to the environment. These could be grouped into four basic temperaments.

# *Know Thyself*

The Myers-Briggs Type Indicator has become a popular tool for determining behavioral patterns. Keirsey and Bates have included in their book a 70-question exercise and a set of answer sheets to help you determine your Myers-Briggs behavior type.

Other systems also divide human behavior into four categories. One of the more popular is the Performax Personal Profile System, copyrighted by Performax Systems International, Inc. Many personnel departments and training organizations administer the Performax Personal Profile System.

Performax divides us all into behavior styles that it identifies through the acronym DISC. They are:

** Dominant

** Interacting

** Steady

** Cautious.

Behind each of these labels is a complex behavioral pattern through which we view the world and respond to it. All of us incorporate the four behavior styles in one combination or another. We differ in the degree to which we prefer one style over the others. Performax therefore subdivides our behavior into "classical patterns" that represent different combinations of the core styles. But for the purpose of simplicity, we'll deal with the core styles.

Why is it important to know your behavior style?

Because your behavior style is a good predictor of your chances of success in a given calling. If you're a house cat, you don't want to go out chasing foxes; if you're a dairy cow, you don't want to find yourself hitched to a plow; if you love to interact with other people, you don't want to be tied to a desk in an isolated office; if you love to work with ideas, but hate conflict, you are more likely to succeed as a writer than as a lawyer or politician. You want to find a calling that will allow you to give free rein to your natural inclinations. I have a natural thirst for knowledge and an outgoing nature. Education was the ideal field for me. But a person who loves the outdoors or who loves to work with tools instead of with ideas might find the teaching profession a sentence to misery.

Let's look at the four basic behavior styles and see how they might relate to career choices.

# HIGH D

Let's begin with the "High D" personality. The "High D" is better at leading than at following; better at giving orders than at taking them. High D's often rise to positions of corporate leadership. They are the movers and shakers.

High D people have strong egos. They are driven by a will to win and by a fear of losing. Their attitude is exemplified by Vince Lombardi's famous motto: "Winning isn't everything; it's the only thing." This hunger for victory often makes them seem insensitive to others. It isn't that High D's are incapable of love; it's just that they have a fear of appearing soft. "Softness" is equated with weakness, and weakness doesn't produce winners. So the High D may subscribe to Leo Durocher's theory: "Nice guys finish last." In the mind of the High D, being nice isn't what wins friends; being first is what does it. High D's fear that if they become losers, nobody will love them.

High D's have many traits that equip them for leadership. They are good long-range planners. They like to visualize the big picture and let their subordinates fill in the details. That means they are also good delegators. The High D will set a goal, point subordinates toward that goal, then go off in search of other worlds to conquer.

High D's are excellent idea people, but if there's no one to whom they can delegate the implementation, they may walk away from their ideas. They become bored with routine and go off looking for other challenges.

High D's are the people who keep their cool during emergencies. In the midst of a crisis, when others are losing their heads, the High D will take charge and lead the way out of the situation.

High D people are not philosophizers. They are left-brain people who reason in straight lines, from generalities to specifics. They don't want to be bothered by a lot of whys and what-ifs. It's "what is" that counts, and the High D is good at taking "what is" and turning it into "what can be."

High D's like to be complimented, but they want to be complimented on what they accomplish and not on what nice people they are. Tell a High D, "You did a great job" and watch the proud smile. Say, "You're a terrific person," and the pride will turn to embarrassment.

When High D's get angry, everyone knows it. They don't stew inwardly; they ventilate their feelings. This may take some understanding on the part of their associates. High D's are not trying to intimidate people and they don't necessarily mean to offend. They often are unaware of the effects of their words and actions on the feelings of others. It's just their way of getting things off their chests.

If you recognize these High D traits in yourself, you can use them to guide you in choosing a career and in making the most of yourself in whatever career you pursue.

If you're a High D, you probably won't be at your best in a career that places you under close supervision. You should look instead for a position that allows you considerable leeway for decision-making. You want a job in which your supervisor can give you broad guidelines, then step back and let you get the results.

You will also chafe at a job that requires you to keep up with petty details. But you will excel at a job that calls for aggressive competition. Your love for victory will propel you to success, and will be an asset to the organization for which you work.

Being aware of your High D tendencies may help you in your interpersonal relationships. Remember that others may misunderstand your motives when you go all-out to win. Take a little time to understand the feelings of your associates who follow the other behavior styles. You don't have to change your basic behavior style; just develop a little more tolerance for the styles of others.

Remember also that to succeed you have to finish what you start. As a High D, you have a tendency to seek new challenges before you've had a chance to master old ones. High D's often find themselves taking on more tasks than they can handle. They're like jugglers who keep trying to take on more balls. When they finally have more balls than they can keep in the air, they drop them all and go looking for more balls. If you have that tendency, you'll have to do one of two things: Discipline yourself to take on no more than you can handle, or look for ways to delegate.

# HIGH I

The High I is the interacting socializer. Like High D's, the High I's are extroverts, but the I's are more people-oriented. They love to be around people, and they love to be admired and liked by people. Whereas the High D is motivated by a hunger for victory, the High I is motivated by a hunger for applause. For the High D, it's the result that counts. For the High I, it's the performance that counts. High D's like to direct people. High I's prefer to influence them. The High D might say, "Do what I say because I'm the boss." The High I would be more likely to say, "Do what I want you to do because you like me."

High I's, like their "D" cousins, prefer to work with the big picture. They are impatient with details. They are prone to jump off the deep end without looking where they're going to land. They don't like to analyze. They trust their intuitions, and so will bet the farm on their gut decisions.

The adventurous I's are often overconfident. Give them driving lessons, and they'll be ready to take on the Los Angeles freeways the first time behind the wheel and will be eager to put the car into a four-wheel drift, especially if there's an audience. After all, they've seen Steve McQueen do it.

High I's crave the limelight, but there's a flip side to that: They fear public embarrassment. Dressing down an I person in public is a sure way to destroy the individual's self-esteem.

High I's, therefore, will go to great lengths to avoid looking foolish. They are poor time managers and often take on more than they can handle. But to avoid looking foolish, they'll go to great lengths to finish a job on time. They're good at last-minute assignments.

High I's, though, do not like stressful situations. Confronted with such situations, they're likely to walk away.

If you're an I person in search of a suitable career, look for something that allows you to interact with people. And look for a job that will exploit your innate talents. I'm a High I, and I've followed careers that allow me to exploit my love for learning while interacting with other people. Find the job that suits your talents and inclinations and you'll be spurred on by applause from your associates. Look for a position that puts you in side-by-side competition with others, too. Friendly competition can be a great incentive for the High I. I was great friends with Anne Mallard in high school, but she was more than a friend. She offered me the challenge of competition. I finished ahead of her in the Voice of Democracy contest. She nosed me out for salutatorian honors. We both benefited from the competition.

As a high I, you wouldn't want a job that required you to work alone. As a lighthouse keeper, you'd be climbing the walls. As a tour guide, you'd be in your element. Find something that lets you indulge your natural love for people.

If you're a High I, you don't tolerate boredom well, and complexities bore you. So look for a job that will enable you to deal with the big picture and delegate the boring details to others. Look for something that will be constantly stimulating and challenging.

# HIGH S

The High S shares the High I's people-orientation. But this behavior style is more introverted than High D's and High I's. The High I wants to be admired. The High S wants to be liked. Whereas the High I is likely to be flamboyant, even to the point of showboating, the High S is likely to be self-effacing.

The High S is the "nice guy" in the organization. If you want a favor done, ask Mr. "S." He'll do it just so you'll continue to like him. If it's a dirty job, but *somebody* has to do it, assign it to Ms. S. She'll do it out of her strong sense of duty.

The S behavior style is the one most likely to work smoothly with other behavior styles.

High S people like harmony and stability. They dislike conflict and change. As supervisors, they don't issue orders. They make requests.

High S people make good team players. Their innate loyalty serves them well. To them, personal glory is secondary to the common goal. You won't catch a High S baseball player swinging for the fences when the situation calls for a bunt.

The High D is motivated by the will to win. The High I is motivated by the opportunity to shine. The High S is motivated by a desire to serve. By serving others, the High S wins their approval and affection.

Although High S individuals like people, they are also capable of performing well in isolation. They are good at logical reasoning and are sticklers for procedure. If you want it done right, give a High S some step-by-step instructions. The job will be done by the book.

If you're a High S you may want to look into careers that enable you to help others. A High S might make a good school teacher, a good doctor or a good counselor. You might want to think twice before entering a pursuit that requires bold, decisive decision-making. You might also want to avoid callings that require you to administer discipline. As a High S, you don't like to crack the whip. You'd rather be liked than to be obeyed.

That doesn't mean that a High S is unqualified for an executive position. But if you go into an executive position, be sure it's one you can handle without departing from your behavior style.

If you want a contrast between executive styles, take a look at two American generals: George Patton and Dwight Eisenhower.

Patton was the impulsive risk-taker, the brilliant, go-for-the-jugular tank commander. He could "smell a battlefield," and once he set his mind on an objective he was impatient with those who counseled caution or a "go-slow" approach. Patton was not a team player. He wasn't a part of the show; he WAS the show. He was undoubtedly a High D.

Eisenhower was the easy-going S. The story is told about the time Eisenhower, then an Army colonel, took flight lessons from a first lieutenant. When he made an unsatisfactory landing, the junior officer gave him a severe dressing-down and asked, "What's your excuse, colonel?"

Eisenhower meekly responded, "No excuse."

Yet it was the steady Eisenhower, not the impulsive Patton, who was chosen as Supreme Allied Commander in Europe. Why? Because the task called for a team player—a person who could work smoothly with British, American and free French political and military leaders; who could deal with the unpredictable Patton and the egotistical Bernard Montgomery; who could bide his time until the American industrial establishment could produce the landing craft necessary to launch the greatest invasion in history.

When action was required, Patton was your man. When careful planning was required, Eisenhower was your man.

Was Ike therefore incapable of making a major decision?

No. When the time for D-Day arrived, Eisenhower faced a dilemma. The weather had been stormy, which made beach assaults in the Normandy area unthinkable. But a weather report came in. There was a good chance that favorable weather conditions would give the allies a narrow window of opportunity. Should they take the risk?

Relying not on his gut but on a careful analysis of the available information, Eisenhower made the decision: Go. And he dictated a memorandum accepting full responsibility for the decision. The High S made a good decision. And he did it without departing from his behavior style.

If you review the material in Chapter Two, you'll note the importance of the team approach in the business organization of the future. Corporations will be needing the team skills of the High S.

If you're a High S you can take advantage of this demand for your kind of temperament. But remember, too, that risk-taking will also be a sought-after characteristic of the 21st century executive. The 21st century will be a century of change. If you're a High S, be prepared for this and learn to adapt to change.

Remember too that it doesn't hurt occasionally to toot your own horn. As a High S, you don't like to go to the boss and ask for a raise. You want to be recognized and rewarded for your achievements without having to ask for the recognition and rewards. But occasionally, you need to speak up.

# HIGH C

High C's, like High S's, are introverts. But High C's are not driven by a desire to be liked. They do not work for the approval and admiration of others. They set their own standards of achievement, and bend their efforts toward meeting those standards. Their standards are usually quite high. High C's tend to be perfectionists. They are impatient with imperfection in themselves and in others.

The High C doesn't need the company of others to do a good job. If you're someone who can spend long hours in a lonely laboratory or studio or office working on a complex problem that requires minute attention to detail, you're no doubt a High C.

High C's aim for quality and consistency. More than any other behavior style, they become involved in detail. The contrast can be observed in the executive styles of two recent presidents: Jimmy Carter and Ronald Reagan.

Carter, the High C with his engineer's training, was a hands-on president, deeply involved with the details of national policy. It was he who brought Menachem Begin and Anwar Sadat to Camp David, where he personally mediated the Camp David Accords that removed the enmity between Israel and Egypt. But Carter, the technician, was unable to exert the personal persuasion needed to rally the country behind his policies.

Reagan, the High I, was impatient with the details of the office. He left it to the White House staff and to his Cabinet to implement the details of policy and diplomacy. But he was a cheerleader *par excellence.* No one was better than Reagan at rallying the country behind his policies.

If you're a High C, you are a cautious decision-maker. You are willing to act only after you're sure of all your facts. If you're working with a lot of High D's and High I's, this quality will infuriate them. They'll be demanding action while you'll be holding off until you're absolutely sure that you're doing the right thing.

The meticulous qualities of the perfectionist High C can be valuable in many pursuits. If you're going to undergo open-heart surgery, you might be reassured to know that the person holding the scalpel will be a High C. You'll want High C's doing the maintenance and performing the pre-flight checks on the aircraft you'll be flying.

If your income-tax form is a complicated one, a High C is the person you'll want to prepare it for you. If you're involved in a complex lawsuit, the High C lawyer is the one most likely to prepare a strong case based upon the law. (If you're a fan of the television series "LA Law," you might find it fun to guess the behavior styles of the different lawyers in the firm.)

If you're a high C, look for a career that will reward those who can handle complexities well and who excel at meticulous detail. You will probably be uncomfortable in a career that calls for quick, gut decisions based upon an intuitive reading of the situation.

We all represent different combinations of the four basic styles. We may even follow different styles in different situations. You may be a High I when dealing with your peers and a High S when dealing with your boss. When dealing with subordinates, the D component may be more pronounced, although it's unlikely that a person will be a consistent High S in one role and a consistent High D in another.

# RUN WITH THE WIND

The important thing to remember is that over the long haul, our behavior styles remain fairly constant. We should therefore look for roles that will enable us to function well without consistently departing from our core styles.

We can divide your possible roles into three categories: Downwind pursuits, leeward pursuits and upwind pursuits.

Downwind pursuits are those ideally suited for your behavior style. When you enter such a pursuit, you naturally go into it full steam ahead. It is as natural to you as swimming is to a fish; as flying is to a sparrow. The wind is at your back, and this is the calling in which you are most likely to succeed.

Leeward pursuits may not come so naturally, but you can pick up the knowledge and skills you need fairly easily. Although the tasks don't exhilarate you, they don't depress you either. The wind isn't at your back, but it isn't blowing against you. You are likely to do quite well in such pursuits.

Upwind pursuits are those that require you to step entirely outside of your behavior style. Going to work is like putting on a hair shirt. Getting ahead is like pedaling a bicycle against the wind. You will end up expending a great deal of energy but without commensurate rewards. Avoid upwind pursuits.

# THE ANIMAL SCHOOL

Unfortunately, many people get trapped into competing in areas for which they are naturally unsuited. Sometimes they do it under pressure from parents, peers or bosses. Even the educational system has been known to push children toward more prestigious careers, for which they were not suited by temperament or talent, instead of toward other careers in which their talents and temperaments might have carried them to success.

I'm indebted to Dr. G. H. Reeves, assistant superintendent of Cincinnati Public Schools, for the fable of The Animal School, which beautifully illustrates this point.

It seems that the leaders of the animal world decided that they should do something to meet the problems of "a new world." So they organized a school.

Since success in the animal world requires well-developed motor skills, the curriculum consisted of running, climbing, swimming and flying. To make it easier to administer the curriculum, all the animals took all the subjects.

The mallard was excellent in swimming; in fact, she could swim like a duck. But she made only passing grades in flying and was very poor in running. Since she was so slow afoot, she had to stay after school to practice. But she still couldn't keep up with a beagle, much less a greyhound, so she was forced to drop swimming and spend more time on running. The extra running was hard on her webbed feet. They became so worn that the mallard became only mediocre at swimming. But average was acceptable in school, so nobody worried about that except the duck.

The rabbit started at the top of the class in running. But he was barely able to keep afloat in swimming and had to do so much make-up work that he had a nervous breakdown.

The squirrel was excellent in climbing and might have been passable in flying class, but the teacher made her start from the ground up instead of from the treetop down. The squirrel developed a charlie horse from over-exertion. This resulted in a C in climbing and a D in running. And of course she flunked flying.

The eagle was a problem child and was disciplined severely. In the climbing class, he beat all the others to the top of the tree, but he insisted on getting there his own way instead of the textbook way.

At the end of the year, an abnormal eel that could swim exceedingly well and also run, climb and fly a little, had the highest average and was valedictorian.

The prairie dogs stayed out of school and fought the tax levy because the administration would not add digging and burrowing to the curriculum. They apprenticed their children to a badger and later joined the groundhogs and gophers to start a successful private school.

Does this fable have a moral?

You bet it does. Any program that forces people to perform tasks for which they are naturally unsuited will fail—and it will damage the people involved. Any program that teaches people to exploit their natural abilities will succeed—and will produce a crop of winners.

## UNDERSTANDING OTHERS

By getting to know yourself, you will obtain an invaluable fringe benefit. You will come to know others better as well.

The important thing to remember is that behavior styles cannot be classified as "good" or "bad." They are simply different, and those differences are what makes the world so interesting.

Suppose you were going to build a house. You might want a High S for an architect. The High S would be eager to produce a design that pleased you, and not necessarily one that pleased the architect. You might want a High D for a builder. The High D would keep all the subcontractors in line and would keep the project moving toward completion. You might want a High C in charge of the electrical system, the plumbing and the interior finishing. You also might want a High C doing the final inspection. When it comes to interior decorations, you might turn to a High I for brightness and flair. Each behavior style would be making a valuable and vital contribution toward your enjoyment of your home.

The same goes for every other human pursuit. Each behavior style has a contribution to make.

But each behavior style also has its down side. If you're a High D, you may be impatient with the methodical pace of the High C. If you're a High I, you may want to prod the High S to be more innovative and more accepting of change. If you're a High S, you may find the High I's frenetic pace exhausting, and the High D's relish for competition a bit intimidating.

When we understand that the people close to us are acting in harmony with their core styles, then it becomes easier for us to accept them. Instead of saying, "Don is a tyrant who has no regard for other people's feelings," we might say, "Don is a High D, and he's afraid we'll perceive him as being too soft. Let's look for ways to help him direct his energy toward team goals. That way, we can help him win and he'll help us to win."

This ability to recognize behavior styles and to motivate the people who follow each style will be an invaluable asset in the work place of the 21st century. Remember, the successful executive of the future will be a person who leads and inspires, not one who orders and intimidates.

Learn to understand and motivate others, and you will have acquired an important success skill for the future.

The learning process should start with you. Know yourself. To your own self be true. And it must follow, as night follows day, that you can't be false to anyone.

# Chapter Five
## *Acquire Balance*

*Fortunate, indeed, is the man who takes exactly the right measure of himself, and holds a just balance between what he can acquire and what he can use, be it great or be it small.*

*—PETER MERE LATHAM*

The principle of balance is a universal principle. We are just now learning the lesson that to live comfortably on the earth, we have to strike a balance, not taking from it more than we put back. The same is true of our lives. To prosper, we have to be in harmony with our fellow humans, with our natural environment, and with ourselves. We achieve that balance by practicing love toward our fellow inhabitants of this planet, toward the planet itself and, importantly, toward ourselves.

# PROSPERITY IS MORE THAN YOUR BANK BALANCE

As we have seen, no individual can make it alone. We prosper with the help of others. But just as we benefit from the efforts of others, so others must benefit from our efforts. We get from life what we put into life. That's the immutable law of balance.

No matter how much we value our rugged individualism, we function as part of a system. To achieve maximum prosperity, we have to be in balance with the system. Put a load of clothes in the washing machine and let them become unbalanced—all the weight on one side—and see what happens during the spin cycle. The machine would shake itself to pieces were it not for the switch that automatically cuts it off when the load becomes unbalanced.

Our lives can become unbalanced too, if we let our priorities get out of balance, if we fail to give proper weight to the things that count, and if we fail to contribute our fair share to the relationships, the communities and the organizations that form the structures of our lives.

Balance is necessary to prosperity. Prosperity is not something that can be measured in bank balances, salaries or net-worth statements. When you have material abundance but are spiritually destitute, you are not really prosperous. Billions of dollars in assets will bring no pleasure when your health has been spent beyond retrieval.

True contentment is essential to prosperity, and true contentment implies a condition of healthy balance.

True prosperity requires that we be balanced in these four areas of health:

** Physical

** Emotional and mental

** Social

** Spiritual.

# PHYSICAL HEALTH

As already noted, physical health was a gift my parents bestowed, not just through the genes they bequeathed me but through the healthy farm lifestyle they insisted that I follow.

Physical health, of course, requires a balance in many areas.

It requires a nutritional balance. It requires a balance between exercise and rest. It requires a balance between work and recreation. It requires a balance between waking and sleeping.

# NUTRITIONAL BALANCE

Nutritional balance was not a thing we had to worry about a great deal on the farm. Mama didn't have to worry much about the nutritional values of the fruits, vegetables and grains we harvested on the farm. These were the foods God meant us to eat, and we ate them—naturally. We picked the beans from our fields, we shelled them, and we cooked them. We dug and peeled the sweet potatoes, harvested and shucked the corn. No preservatives were added.

We drank milk from the cow and water from a well, purified by nature's own filtering process.

We ate meat from the animals we slaughtered—hams cured in our own smokehouse, sausage we ground ourselves, with seasonings added to suit our own taste.

We spent our days in healthy labor, which did wonders for the appetite. After we had worked all day in the field, Mama didn't lavish us with junk food. We ate the hearty, wholesome fruits of our labors.

Today, many of our national health problems can be attributed to poor nutrition. Poor nutrition, in turn, is often a product of depression. Depression is often a product of humdrum lives, devoid of meaningful work. Americans fight blues and boredom by stuffing themselves. Then they become overweight and go on diets to regain their trim figures.

This is not balanced nutrition. It is alternating between two imbalances. People become overbalanced and gorge themselves. Seeing the consequence of this imbalance, they proceed to starve themselves. They never seem to achieve a healthy balance.

The pursuit of the willowy form has brought on its own kind of imbalance. Children as young as fourth-graders have been found to be dieting to lose weight.

I don't mean to suggest that to achieve the physical health necessary for true prosperity you need to duplicate the dietary habits of a Southern farm family of the '40s and '50s. I subscribe to Ed Foreman's formula for daily food intake: 25% at breakfast, 50% at lunch and 25% at dinner—or supper—before 7 P.M.

Sensible eating habits are necessary to good health. If your daily diet consists of a sweet bun and black coffee for breakfast, a Big Mac and milkshake for lunch and Pizza and Pepsi for dinner, you're out of balance. If you're packing in the nachos, cheese cake and candy bars between meals, you're out of balance.

When you subject your body to that kind of imbalance, you are handicapping yourself in the arena of success. You cannot devote your full energy to meeting career challenges when your body has to divert so much of it to redressing these imbalances.


# EXERCISE AND REST

Physical health also requires a balance between exercise and rest. Back on the farm, we didn't worry about whether we got enough exercise. During school months, there were plenty of chores to keep our bodies busy, both before and after school. During summer "vacation" from school, there was work to be done in the fields. Nobody ever accused us of leading sedentary lives.

It's amazing how times have changed since then. We have developed mechanical and electronic devices to wait on us hand and foot. A large portion of Americans spend their days in pursuits that require little muscular exercise. Then we go home and relax in front of the television set. Our muscles grow flabby, our bodies grow sluggish, and we become—to borrow from Hippocrates—phlegmatic.

Not everyone, of course, goes home and collapses in front of the TV. Millions of Americans have taken up some form of exercise, which is healthy—if you keep it in balance.

Exercise not only tones up your muscles and keeps your heart in shape, but also promotes a healthy feeling of well-being. When you exercise, you stimulate your body's production of endorphins, substances that act on certain sensors in the brain to produce a mild euphoria.

Unfortunately, many people become addicted to these "endorphin highs," and become exercise fanatics. They push their bodies to the limit, often bringing on muscle problems and heart trouble. You don't need a rigorous exercise regimen to stay healthy. Twenty minutes of brisk walking or the equivalent three or four times a week will keep most people fit. I use a 15- to 20-minute exercise routine in the morning to wake me up and get my blood circulating. I've discovered that a lifetime membership in a health spa is not the answer. You don't need expensive equipment to stay in shape. All you need is enough space to lie down on the floor and exercise.

## WORK AND RELAXATION

Good physical health also requires a balance between work and relaxation. Work is good for us. It gives us a sense of usefulness. People who inherit large fortunes and spend their lives in idle pursuits are not truly happy. Nor can they be said to be truly prosperous. They are parasites, not producers.

People locked into the welfare cycle, who live off government doles, are not truly happy, and they certainly aren't prosperous.

Active people who retire soon find that complete leisure isn't all it's cracked up to be. Those who live long, healthy lives find active pursuits even in retirement.

I have encountered a number of senior citizens who have found healthy outlets for their energy through volunteerism. Among them was a woman in her 80s who liked to go into the schools and read to the pupils. She particularly liked the kindergarten and first-grade classes, and she told me about one student who came up to hug her at the end of the school year.

"I'll love you until you turn into a skeleton," the child said.

Such activities—and such a response—help keep active seniors healthy and productive long after their less-active contemporaries have retired to their rocking chairs or have passed on to their rewards.

Work, then, is a healthy activity for all ages. It is particularly healthy when it's the kind of work you enjoy doing.

## A TIME FOR OTHER THINGS

But there comes a time when you need to turn your attention away from the job and let your mind and body renew themselves. The balanced individual doesn't allow the job to be the all-consuming passion in life. There must also be time for friends, family—and oneself.

A good hobby is an excellent way to give yourself a rest from the cares of the daily grind. Generally, it's best if the hobby is not related to your job. If you make your living as a cabinet-maker, you probably wouldn't want to take up woodworking as a hobby. You might want to try photography, or music. The writer or accountant or salesperson, though, might enjoy woodworking. If you spend your days in strenuous physical exertion, you might not want to take up a vigorous hobby such as tennis. You might look for a quieter, more relaxing pursuit.

The idea is to balance your working day with some activity that will provide a pleasant and relaxing contrast. It should be something you do simply because you enjoy doing it and not because it produces some product or achieves some goal.

# TAKE CONTROL OF YOUR TIME

Balanced individuals take control of their time. They do not become slaves of the clock or the calendar. They don't go around lamenting, "I don't have time to do all the things I have to do."

Nobody gets more than 24 hours in a given day. All of us have to fit our lifetimes into those 24-hour units. Don't try to do more than you can reasonably do in that time. If you try to squeeze 26 hours' worth of activity into every 24-hour period, you'll end up exhausted and nonproductive.

Don't let others control your time. Many of us feel guilty when we have to say "no" to a request for our time. When somebody asks us for a favor that robs us of time we need for ourselves, we are prone to say "yes" anyway. We allow people to drop in for a chat when we have pressing matters to take care of. We allow people to call us on business during the hours we've set aside for ourselves and our families. We do it because we want to be nice.

Well, you can be nice and still be fair to yourself. Educate your friends and associates to your need to control your time. If they're real friends, they'll understand and will respect you.

If you find yourself burdened with more duties than you can comfortably take care of, examine your priorities. There may be some obligations you need to shed. It is good to find ways of making contributions to your community, but these contributions have to be kept in balance with other demands on your time.

Many busy people have found that the secret to accomplishing a great deal without surrendering control of their time is to delegate. This can be done at work, where you can teach others how to do some of the things you do. And it can be done at home, where you can delegate chores to children, thereby teaching them responsibility while relieving some of the stress on your time.

Remember that some things are more important than others. Many of us are perfectionists who believe that anything worth doing is worth doing right. But with some things, perfection isn't worth the time it takes to achieve it. If you're typing up a shopping list, you don't have to be sure the margins are set correctly, margarine is spelled with only one "e," and Jell-O is capitalized in both places. It doesn't matter. If you're typing the copy for an advertising proposal, it's important. But for a shopping list, it isn't.

Whatever the demands of your time, be sure you schedule some "retreat time" each day. Let that be your time to do whatever you want to do. If you just want to put your feet up, close your eyes and relax, do it, and don't feel guilty about it. It's part of the balance you need to put into every day of your life.

# WAKING AND SLEEPING

You also need a balance between waking and sleeping. Individuals vary in the amount of sleep they need, but seven or eight hours a night seems to be the happy medium. If you get too little sleep, you will be too tired and drowsy to perform at peak energy during the day. If you get too much sleep, you will be sluggish and listless. And of course the time spent in bed is time taken away from hobbies, family, friends and pleasurable activities.

# EMOTIONAL AND MENTAL HEALTH

Emotional and mental health are closely related to physical health. Emotional distress can lead to physical illness and physical illness can lead to emotional distress. It has been estimated that 50% to 90% of all physical disorders in the United States are related to stress.

Balanced individuals learn to deal with the stress in their lives. They look for career opportunities that allow them to "be themselves"—to function within their behavior styles.

# INTERPERSONAL RELATIONSHIPS

Mental and emotional balance also requires a balance in our interpersonal relationships. We must be able to relate harmoniously with our fellow humans; otherwise, we set ourselves up for unnecessary bouts of stress and for the physical ailments that accompany stress.

On the job, a tolerance for the behavior styles of others can be of immense help in fostering smooth relations. A knowledge of the behavior styles makes it possible for you to practice the Golden Rule in spirit and not just in the letter. If you are a High D, it might not be enough to do unto others as you would have others do unto you. Suppose the "others" are High S's. What would be pleasing to you might be offensive to them. So to practice the spirit of the rule, you would want to do unto others as you would have others do unto you *if you followed their behavior style.*

# FAMILY RELATIONSHIPS

On-the-job relationships are not the only ones that are important to your prosperity. Balanced family relationships are vital if you expect to be all that you can be.

We have already seen how dramatically the family has changed over the past 30 or 40 years. More than 95% of the households in America differ from the "traditional" household in which the husband is the provider while the wife stays home to keep house and care for the children.

This change in the typical family has resulted in a change in the balance of relationships among family members. If both husband and wife work outside the home, how will they share the responsibilities in the home that were once shouldered exclusively by the wife? If the family constitutes a single-parent household, how does it compensate for the role of the missing parent?

These questions have complex answers. Obviously, when both spouses hold jobs outside the home, they need to arrive at a mutual understanding of how the responsibilities will be divided and how the financial burden will be shared. But, just as important, each must be aware of the other's emotional needs, and each must see that those needs are taken care of. A relationship in which one spouse is the giver and the other is the taker is an unbalanced relationship.

When there's only one parent in the house, the children may have to shoulder heavier responsibilities than might be the case in two-parent households.

## THE FAMILY MOBILE

A family is like a hanging mobile. Each member is like an element suspended from an arm of the mobile. Each is necessary to maintain the balance. When one element changes, the mobile becomes unbalanced. The others have to adjust to compensate.

Often this changes comes in the form of destructive behavior by one member of the family. A spouse may become emotionally unbalanced or may become addicted to drugs or alcohol. The family mobile is out of balance. The other elements tend to compensate. If the husband is the one with the destructive behavior, the wife may assume the responsibility for earning a living, disciplining the children, and all the other duties a husband might normally be expected to carry out. Sometimes an older child assumes the role of the irresponsible parent.

Often, the whole family lifestyle is orchestrated around the problem behavior. Other family members are trying to control the problem person by adopting compensating behavior of their own. This condition has been labeled "codependence," and it represents an unbalanced state of affairs. Although the objective is to restore balance to the family mobile, individual family members are forced to become unbalanced with relation to the rest of the world. When one member of a family becomes unbalanced, the wise course is to bring that member back into balance, perhaps through family counseling or therapy. It is never a sound practice to throw others in the family out of balance.

The problem may appear to lie in the behavior of one family member, but the root may lie in the dynamics of the family. Therefore, it is important that all members of the family participate in the counseling. One member can't be "fixed" and sent back into the family with the expectation that the problem has been solved. Even if only one member is absent from the counseling, the whole situation hasn't been addressed. Every member of the family contributes in some degree to the balance or imbalance of the whole.

# FOUR WINNING PRINCIPLES FOR PARENTS

Our relationship with our children always requires a balance of gentleness and firmness—both of which are expressions of love when appropriately applied. It is critical that children know what behavior is expected of them.

I have four principles for guiding children toward productive behavior:

**\*\*** Develop responsibility. To do this, you must do more than talk about it. You have to exemplify it. Instead of criticizing your child's behavior, improve on your own. That takes effort. I know, because I have to pay constant attention to my tendency to fuss too much. I tend to say "don't" more often than I say "do." If you let children know what they're *supposed* to do, you will find them less inclined to do what they're *not* supposed to do.

Never do for children what they can do for themselves. Parents who are overly responsible often produce irresponsible children. When you assume your childrens' responsibilities, you deprive them of opportunities to learn. Most adults underestimate the abilities of their children. For example, homework is your child's responsibility. Stay out of it except to answer questions or give suggestions. Homework is their assignment, not yours. If your child doesn't do the assigned homework, there will be consequences to suffer at school.

Don't bribe your child to make good grades, and don't act betrayed if the report card is not all A's and B's. It's no disgrace to make a C, and C students shouldn't be made to feel like pariahs. When your child brings in a bad report card, have a five-minute talk in private. Don't overreact. Ask what the child has to say about it and what he plans to do about it, and go from there.

** Give encouragement. Encouragement is essential in winning children over. Encouragement implies faith in and respect for your children *as they are*. The basic goal of all humans is to fit in; to belong; to find their respective places in society. This goal can be achieved if three basic needs can be met. We each need to love, to be loved, and to know we're loved. Encouragement tells us we're loved, and knowing we're loved helps us to reciprocate the love. Encouragement is not the same thing as praise. You give praise when a task is completed or something is done well. You give encouragement even when the child fails.

I saw the value of encouragement demonstrated in the case of Larry, a student in that class in Columbia that I sent to the restrooms for a reading lesson. Larry was a problem student. I executed a lot of behavioral-management strategies in that class, and even after a week or so, Larry still hadn't settled into a routine. I responded in a way that puzzled Larry. Instead of yelling and screaming, I would lower my voice. One day Larry said to me, "Mrs. O'Tuel, I can tell you haven't been teaching long. You haven't learned to scream yet."

I decided that Larry wasn't going to learn much from a textbook. So I got a motorcycle handbook and a driver's handbook, and we did a lot of nontraditional things to stimulate learning.

At that time, I made a practice of making four calls a week to the parents of my students. I would call the parents of two students who had shown the most improvement and two who needed to make some improvements. I called Larry's home on a Friday night. I wanted his mother to know that Larry had finally stayed in his seat for at least 15 minutes and had completed an assigned task. I knew his mother worked late, so I called about 11 P.M. Larry answered.

"Larry, may I speak to your mother?" I asked.

"She's not here," he said.

"That's too bad, Larry. I wanted to tell her that you were able to stay on task today and complete your assignment; I'm really proud of you."

"Wait a minute," said Larry. "I think she just came through the door."

When I gave Larry's mother the good news, there was a long silence. Then I heard sobs.

"You know, Mrs. O'Tuel," she said, "Larry's been going to school for 10 years. This is the first time anybody has ever called me and told me something *good* about him."

That little gesture of encouragement was something Larry and his mother badly needed. If Larry had not heard an encouraging word in 10 years of school, no wonder he was a behavioral problem. Show me a misbehaving child and I'll show you a discouraged child. Study after study has revealed that school and self-concept go hand in hand. By giving generous portions of responsibility and encouragement to our children, we go a long way toward helping them build a positive self-image.

** Administer discipline. Note that I said "discipline" and not "punishment." Discipline is best achieved when we don't confuse it with reward and punishment. I recommend the use of logical and natural consequences in discipline. Tongue-lashings do not constitute effective discipline. It's better to act than to talk. Talking provides an opportunity for arguments, and you can lose an argument. Your child knows what's wrong, so you waste your time when you preach. Reward and punishment are not effective. When you reward children, they learn to do things for the wrong reason. They learn the profit motive instead of the love motive. Punishment tells your children something is wrong with them. It hurts; it's a put-down. When you punish your children, you discourage them and develop resistance in them. Inflicting pain invites bitterness and instills a desire for retaliation. It does not stimulate cooperation.

When children misbehave, don't ask them why. They rarely are aware of the real purpose of their behavior. Ask them what happened and what they can do differently in the future to prevent it from happening again. Ask what you can do to help, and go from there. Look for ways to encourage your child.

** Have fun together. Remember what it's like to be a kid. Develop a relationship based on mutual respect, love and affection, mutual confidence and trust, and a feeling of belonging. Play together, work together, laugh together and seek out experiences in which you have to cooperate.

Speak to your child the way you would speak to a friend. Tape your talking. Are you always nagging, scolding, preaching or correcting? Don't try to settle your problems while you're both hot under the collar. Let things cool off, then try to reach a solution. Stop irritating your children and make friends with them. Remember: You are a morale officer in your home. If you want to know what kind of parents your kids will make, take a look at yourself. You're teaching them the art of being a parent.

Set aside some time each week to do something special with each child. Cultivate a positive, warm and lasting relationship. Don't assume that because you were a child once you understand what your children are going through. Times have changed. And no two childhoods are exactly like. Once, when I told my younger son, Bryant, that I knew what it was like to be a child, he replied: "But you don't know what it's like to be the second son." And he was right.

# FAMILY COMMUNICATIONS

The ability to communicate is one of the most vital skills in keeping a family in healthy balance.

I have worked with troubled youth for many years now, and over and over I hear them say that a major problem in their lives is poor communication with their parents. One of the most important sentences in the English language is "What is your opinion?" Try it as an opener with your kids.

Maxcy and I have found that weekly family meetings are helpful in promoting good communications. When our kids were growing up, we would get together each Sunday evening to discuss problems and make plans. We would arrive at decisions all members could live with by giving each member a chance to express opinions and concerns.

When your family life is in balance, you are well on your way to achieving balance in your career, and that balance will help you achieve prosperity.

# SOCIAL HEALTH

A third aspect of health is our social environment. To prosper and be happy, we have to be connected to other people. Successful people are not loners. They have a rich circle of friends and they are involved in their communities.

If you're a person who works from 9 to 5, goes home to dinner, sits in front of the tube from 7 to 11 and sleeps from 11 to 7, it's time to look into your social health.

Socially healthy people are aware of what's happening in the world, the nation, the community and the neighborhood. They exchange information and ideas with a broad range of associates. This information and these ideas provide the foundations for prosperity.

Remember the point made in Chapter Three: There's no such thing as a self-made person. You need a network of friends to encourage you, to advise you, to keep you informed, and to put in a good word for you when a good word might help.

How do you find such friends?

By looking for ways to reach out to others. By looking for ways to apply your talents in behalf of your community. Many people make social connections through service clubs such as the Lions Club, Rotary, Sertoma, Civitan, Optimist and Kiwanis. Many become active in churches. I personally have worked with many community-minded people through the Business/Education Partnership program. Through this program, business people volunteer their time and expertise to work with public schools. Some assist in programs to motivate students. Some provide tutoring to students in need of extra help. Some help to develop curricula in specialized areas. Some give classroom presentations. Some become mentors. The possibilities abound.

Some people find excitement and fulfillment in working with volunteer fire departments and rescue squads. Some enjoy coaching community-league athletic teams. Some enjoy the companionship of bridge clubs, reading clubs, photography clubs and other social groups.

The point is that humans are social animals, and to succeed in human society we must cultivate healthy social relationships.

When we belong to a group of like-minded individuals, we find sources of encouragement. Our achievements are applauded, our self-esteem grows and we are motivated toward even greater success.

## SPIRITUAL HEALTH

Many people equate spiritual things with religion. Religion is, indeed, an important aspect of our lives, but spiritual health goes beyond the realm of church attendance.

Spiritual health refers to a healthy involvement with things that touch the inner self in an intuitive, not a logical way. By what logic do we respond to an ode by Keats differently from the way we respond to instructions for assembling a toy? By what logic do we respond to a nocturne by Chopin differently from the way we respond to a policeman's whistle or the first-period bell at school? By what logic do we respond to a movement in "Swan Lake" differently from the way we respond to the movement of a person strolling casually down Main Street?

In a spiritually healthy person, music, dance, and poetry speak to the spirit in the intuitive language of beauty. That doesn't mean that to be spiritually healthy you have to love ballet, enjoy Keats and become rhapsodic over Chopin. But you should be able to experience the beauty of *some* form of music, *some* form of literature and *some* form of the performing arts. If you are lacking in appreciation for the finer things in life, try exposing yourself to them. You may find yourself opening the door to a rich, rewarding dimension to your life.

# THE LAW OF GIVE AND TAKE

Most successful people have mastered an interesting key to prosperity. They've learned that prosperity is closely tied in with giving. Those who give much receive much. Successful people do not go through their lives as takers. They instinctively recognize that there is a balance between giving and receiving.

Healthy communities are those that regularly meet their United Way goals. Healthy businesses are those noted for their corporate generosity as well as the generosity of management and employees. The interesting fact is that most philanthropists were generous *before* they became wealthy.

Generosity is a great booster of self-esteem. The power of the boost is in inverse proportion to the publicity accompanying the gift. Try giving in secret. Ask the recipient not to reveal the source of the generosity. See how good it makes you feel about yourself.

Your generosity, of course, should not be indiscriminate. The best kind of giving is the kind that enables the recipient to become self-sufficient. That was the kind of giving my high-school principal, Charlie Pinner, indulged in when he made that $100 down payment on my education. He knew that once I got under way, there would be no stopping me.

When Charlie Pinner did me that favor, he created a debt for me. It was not a debt to Mr. Pinner; he never expected me to repay that $100 to him. But it was a debt to humanity. Having benefited from his generosity, I was obligated to be generous to others.

The giving doesn't have to be monetary in nature. When we give of our time and expertise, we are contributing toward the good of our fellow man. And it feels wonderful when we do it.

## PRACTICE THE SEVEN L'S

Carolyn Corbin, a futurist, economist and author from Dallas, Texas, has reduced her formula for living to seven L's. The balanced individual will cultivate them. They are:

** Love. David Sugarman says, "Your capacity for happiness is only as great as your ability to give and express love." The first person you have to love is yourself. If you don't love yourself, you can't love others. If you don't feel good about yourself, you can't feel good about the world. And guess what: If you're down on the world, the world will be down on you. You cannot prosper in that kind of world. Many of us go through life with a red-pencil mentality. We're looking for negative things we can check off. Women are particularly susceptible to this mentality. Studies show that we put ourselves down more than men do. For instance, I met a woman once who was wearing a beautiful red blazer she had sewn herself. When I complimented her, she said, "You ought to see the lining." She *had* to find some way to deflect my compliment. Look for the positive in yourself, and when someone compliments you on what you're wearing, say, "Thank you. I like it too!" Loving yourself makes it easier to show love for others. And when you show love for others, they'll reciprocate. Usually. If they hate you in spite of the love you show, love them anyway. It'll make 'em madder than hell. As you practice love toward others, keep in mind the differences among individuals and follow the *spirit* of the Golden Rule: "Do unto others as they would like you to do unto them." When my husband wants to make me happy, he buys me flowers. I love it. When I want to make him happy, do I buy him flowers? Of course not. Flowers are no big deal to Maxcy. What turns him on is a good meal. So when I want to show him how much I love him, I fix a special meal. Find ways to show people you love them. One way is to say so, plainly and directly. Don't be like the old farmer who was talking to a friend about his wife. "Sometimes," he said, "I love Mamie so much it's all I can do to keep from telling her."

** Laughter. Laughter is a skill. Sometimes, as we grow older, we begin to take life very seriously. Life *is* serious business, which is why we are in such great need of laughter to break the tension and infuse joy into our existence. When our older son, William, entered first grade, the teacher said something that made me think. "Send me a happy child in the morning," she said,

"and I will send you a happy child in the afternoon."
I began working on laughter. I found games to play
and songs to sing in the car en route to school, and
all sorts of occasions to bring smiles to the face and
chuckles to the throat. If we make a game of it, we
can find humor in almost any situation. This is especially
true if we learn to laugh at ourselves. A kindergarten
pupil in the Summerville, South Carolina, public-school
system was well on his way to acquiring that skill.
During one show-and-tell session, he had to make a
choice between completing his presentation or going
to the bathroom. He opted to complete his presentation,
and therefore was standing in a puddle at the end of
it. The teacher lovingly took him outside and sought
to ease his embarrassment. She didn't have to. The
child responded with a cool sense of humor. "I only
wet one leg," he said.

** Looking Ahead. As the writer of Proverbs wrote, "Without vision, my people perish." We live in the present,
but the present is just a fleeting moment on the edge
of time. We might compare it to a baseball pitch. First
comes the pitcher's wind-up. Then comes his delivery,
when the ball is launched into its trajectory. Next comes
the arrival at the plate. Then comes the aftermath. We
can look upon the wind-up and the trajectory as the
future. The present is that split-second when the ball
crosses the plate. When you hear the crack of the bat
against the ball—or the pop of the ball striking the
catcher's mitt—you're hearing the sound of the present
turning into the past. When did the batter have an opportunity to control the outcome of the pitch? Not when
the pitch was in the present. By the time the ball was
over the plate, it was too late to get the bat off the
shoulder and swing. Not in the past. When the ball

hits the catcher's mitt, it's either a ball or a strike, and nothing can change it. To control the outcome of that pitch, the batter had to be taking steps while the pitch was still in the future. He had to take his bat off his shoulder when the pitcher went into his wind-up. He had to visualize the path the ball would take. He had to "see" where the bat would be when the ball reached the plate. He had to envision the bat making contact with the ball, driving it to the part of the ballpark where he wanted it to go. And while the ball was still in its trajectory, he had to start his swing so that when it reached the plate—when the present materialized out of the future—the bat would make contact and send the ball into the outfield and maybe out of the park. In our own lives, we have to keep our eyes on the ball—which means on the future. We have to envision the future—which means to see it as if it were already the present. We have to set goals. What do we want to achieve in the future? We have to take appropriate action so that when the future becomes the present, it will be the kind of present we envisioned.

** Learning. Many of us think of learning as something we acquire in schools and in college. Once we have our diplomas in hand, we stop learning and start doing. It doesn't work that way. Learning is a lifelong process. If you had taken a secretarial course in 1950 and learned nothing more after that, where would you be? You wouldn't even be flipping hamburgers, because something has happened since 1950. It's called computerization. The word-processor with its laser printer has replaced the typewriter. The photocopier has replaced the carbon and the stencil. The floppy disc has replaced the manila folder. The fax machine has replaced the telegraph. Go back to Chapter Two. The sum total of human knowledge has been doubling every six years. By the year 2000 it will be doubling every 32 hours. We must learn. We must change, or mediocrity will be the best we can expect.

** Labor. That's an ugly word to a lot of people. We live in an age of leisure. When I was growing up, newspapers did not have "Leisuretime" sections. There was no segment of the economy labeled the "leisure business." Now, says Carolyn Corbin, more than a third of the workers in the work force who are 30 years old and younger are leisure-driven rather than work-driven. That means they're on the job to earn money to pay for whatever they want to do off the job. The job itself is not a source of fulfillment. Instead, it is a means—almost an incidental means—toward off-the-job fulfillment. The leisure ethic has replaced the work ethic. That has to change.

I don't mean to imply that one's whole life has to be wrapped up in work. But can you imagine how the ceiling of the Sistine Chapel might have turned out if Michelangelo's motive had been to earn the money for a ski week-end in the Alps? Can you picture how the American Revolution might have turned out if George Washington's motive had been to protect his hunting and fishing rights at Mount Vernon? Can you imagine trying to read this book at night if Thomas Edison had insisted on a 7-hour day so that he would have plenty of daylight to practice his tennis? The country is not going back to the 72-hour work week, and thank God for that. Nor should we glorify the workaholic as a role model for the 21st century worker. Instead, we need to promote the idea of peak performance. You achieve peak performance by finding a line of work that is meaningful to you, that provides you with fulfillment, and that offers you a chance to put your best talents to their highest use.

** Lifting up. Lifting up means taking a positive view of life. When airline pilots encounter bumpy air, they lift their airplanes over the turbulence. A positive outlook lifts you over the turbulence of life. You actually feel more lighthearted. Your body chemistry changes. You are healthier, more optimistic, and more likely to prosper. You can choose a positive attitude by driving negative thoughts from your mind and replacing them with positive ones. Instead of saying "It's going to be another dreary, rainy day," say, "Boy! I'll bet this rain is going to be great for the daffodils. And it's a perfect opportunity for me to use that bright new umbrella."

** Letting go. Most of us hang on to things we ought to let go of. Fear is among them. Most of the things we're afraid of never happen. As Shakespeare put it, when you're afraid of things in the dark, "How easily is a bush supposed a bear." Or, as Franklin Roosevelt expressed it, "The only thing we have to fear is fear itself." Another thing we need to let go of is worry. Worry is wasted energy. Worrying about what was and what's to come is a sure way to spoil a good day. One way to let go of worry is to find ways to insulate your hot buttons. Find out what really puts you in a frenzy, and avoid those things. I used to think I had to click with every human being I came into contact with. If I had 30 students, I had to succeed with every one. If I had 30 associates, I had to connect with every one. I have learned through the years that my expectations were unrealistic. As you go through life, you'll find that 25% of the people will wish you well no matter what the circumstances. Another 25% will be hoping to see you fall on your face. The remaining 50% don't give a hill of beans what you do. So I don't let myself get worked up because certain people are not bowled over by my charm or because certain problems refuse to yield to my ingenious solutions. Some people go out of their way to be miserable. But we don't have to let them make us miserable. I don't waste my time trying to make friends with alligators, turkeys and frogs; they won't help me and I'm not going to let them hurt me.

We also need to let go of grudges. Aunt Bert never forgave my dad for failing to sell Uncle Thomas' mule after Uncle Thomas died. She wouldn't even speak to him. She would drive into our front yard and honk her horn. Mama would go out there and they would talk. What a waste of energy! For the sake of one sorry old mule, she forfeited years of friendship and companionship. She died an unhappy woman, bereft of friends except for a few saintly souls like my mother. Forgive. Forgive the people who have hurt you or offended you. And most of all, forgive yourself. You are often your toughest critic. Let go. You'll be a happier, more balanced person.

## KEEPING A HAPPY BALANCE

When our lives are in balance, we don't have to spend a lot of time, attention and energy maintaining equilibrium. We tend to stay on course naturally. A child's toy top that is balanced will spin much longer than one that is not balanced. When your automobile tires are balanced, they will last much longer than tires that are unbalanced—and will deliver better gasoline mileage in the bargain.

A recipe with the right balance of salt, sugar and spices will yield a tastier dish than one that is overloaded with one ingredient or the other.

The principle of balance is a universal principle. The seas yield moisture to the air, which turns it into clouds, which pour the rain into the ground. From the ground spring the streams that become rivers that return the water to the seas. Plants breathe the carbon dioxide exhaled by animals and exhale the oxygen that is breathed by animals. Nature is in balance.

We are just now learning the lesson that to live comfortably on the earth, we have to strike a balance, not taking from it more than we put back.

The same is true of our lives. To prosper, we have to be in harmony with our fellow humans, with our natural environment, and with ourselves. We achieve that balance by practicing love toward our fellow inhabitants of this planet, toward the planet itself and, importantly, toward ourselves.

# Chapter Six

# *Become a Good Communicator*

*Speech was made to open man to man, and not to hide him; to promote commerce, and not betray it.*
*—DAVID LLOYD*

*What we've got here is a failure to communicate.*
*—Donn Pearce (in screenplay for "Cool Hand Luke")*

Understanding is the key aim of all communications. You cannot lead or teach or inspire unless you achieve understanding. And understanding is best achieved when there is mutual respect between the transmitter and the receiver of communications. If you respect the people with whom you communicate, you will not try to impress them with how much you know and how little they know. You will approach them at their own level, without appearing to be condescending. You will explain things in terms with which they are familiar.

# EXCHANGING SIGNALS

The leader of tomorrow will be the person who knows how to influence people and inspire them. This will call for communication skills.

The most powerful idea is impotent until it is articulated. The most brilliant order is useless if it is garbled in the transmission. The most beautiful poetry is wasted if it is not understood.

Every human mind is an isolated universe until it exchanges signals with other minds. Fortunately, we are natural communicators. Our minds are constantly sending out signals—some of them conscious and some of them unconscious. They also are constantly receiving signals—sometimes consciously, sometimes unconsciously.

If we are to influence, inspire, and lead, we need to be aware of the signals we are sending, and we need to know how to send them clearly and forcefully.

# COMMUNICATING WITHOUT WORDS

When we think of communications, we usually think of two types: oral and written. But most of our communicating is not done with words. Ninety-three percent of the messages our brains send out to other brains are in non-verbal form. Body language accounts for 55% of our communication. The tone of voice, pace of speech and voice inflections account for 38%.

Because non-verbal communications tend to spring from our subconscious, we are often less aware of them than we are of our verbal communications. Therefore, we tend to exercise less control over non-verbal signals than we do over the words we use. Our body language gives an instant reading on what we mean, before we've had a chance to put a conscious spin on it. That's why people are more likely to believe our non-verbal communications. The idea is expressed in the words of a ballad that was popular when I was young:

> Your lips tell me no no,
> But there's yes, yes in your eyes.

If the lips tell you one thing and the look tells you something else, believe the look.

Someone once came up to me and said, "I didn't dare talk to you last Monday. I saw you whizzing by and I knew something was going on. What were you so upset about?

"Me upset? I didn't say a word!"

"Yes, but your face was angry."

The way you look conveys a powerful message. And the way you look encompasses far more territory than the face.

# THE POWER OF PERSONAL APPEARANCE

Often the first communication others receive from you is in the form of personal appearance. This gives a very powerful first impression of the kind of person you are. It may not be an accurate impression, but it can be potent and lasting.

Just how powerful was born out by an experiment conducted in front of a high-rise office building in a large city on three consecutive days.

On the first day, a man stood outside the building in an expensive-looking business suit. He looked the part of a successful lawyer. As strangers approached he would stop them and say, "Excuse me. I've lost my wallet and I need a couple of dollars to get home."

The typical response was "Oh sure." Some would say, "Take

this five. Buy a newspaper and have a drink on the way home.''
At the end of the day, the man had collected $600.

The next day, the same man appeared in casual clothes—khaki
trousers and a sport shirt. He related the same story. This time the
response was different: "Why don't you call your wife? How could
you do such a stupid thing?" He collected only $139.

The third day, he dressed like a bum. He collected nothing.

The man was sending out different messages by the way he
dressed. On the first day, he was saying, "I am successful. I am
responsible. I am trustworthy.''

On the second day, he was saying, "I'm laid back; I take things
as they come. I'm careless with money.''

On the third day, he was saying, "I'm a failure. I'm irresponsible.
Trust me at your own risk.''

# DRESS FOR INCLUSION, NOT EXCLUSION

If you want your attire to send out a positive message in the
career world, dress to be included, not to be excluded. Observe
what successful people are wearing in the place you want to work.
If you're a woman and the women who seem to have made it are
wearing tailored suits, wear a tailored suit. If they're wearing skirts
and blouses, wear a skirt and blouse. If you're a man and you see
the CEO wearing a three-piece suit, get yourself a three-piece suit.
But be aware that what includes you in one locale may exclude
you in another. The three-piece suit may be the uniform of success
in Boston, but it may be considered stuffy in Fort Worth. String
tie, Western boots and Stetson hat may be your entree to success
in Cowtown, but they will close doors for you in Beantown. Do
your homework.

# CLOTHE YOURSELF IN COMFORT

Dress for comfort. That chic outfit may look great on the slim mannequin in the store, but if it isn't comfortable on you, let the mannequin wear it. People who feel uncomfortable will communicate their feelings through countless non-verbal signals. That expensive hair-do may make you look sultry and sophisticated after five, but if you must constantly be brushing your hair from your eyes, it will be distracting and counter-productive in the working world.

# PUT AUTHORITY AHEAD OF PRICE

Dress for high authority. If you have a choice between buying one expensive suit or three inexpensive ones, buy the expensive one. Buy clothing that won't go out of style. For men, the dark-blue pinstripe suit has demonstrated a lot of staying power. For women, nobody will give you a hard time when you're wearing a beige silk blouse.

The businesswoman should remember that a jacket always adds to your authority. Get an expensive jacket even if you have to buy a much less expensive skirt. What is seen from the waist up is the most important.

Your colors also send out messages: For women, navy, brown, maroon, beige, and jade speak with authority. Solid colors are decisive; plaids and prints are wishy-washy.

Women's accessories also convey different levels of authority. Again the key word is quality. Choose shoes with medium heels. The closed-toe pump, the sling back, and the open toe convey authority in descending order. Earrings and belts provide finishing touches. Wear a belt even when you're wearing a jacket.

Make-up should be traditional and as nearly natural as possible. Too much make-up transmits a negative message. So does no make-up at all.

Be consistent in your dress. Consistency says you're in control of things. If you wear a business suit Monday through Thursday and come in Friday wearing a tee shirt, people will wonder what's up with you.

When you interact with people, go in with a feeling of confidence and optimism. The message they'll get is, "Here's someone worth listening to and worth following."

# THE POSTURE OF PROSPERITY

Your posture is another important way of communicating non-verbally. When you're standing and talking, whether you're conversing with an individual or addressing a group, it's best to stand straight with your weight balanced on the balls of your feet. This conveys the impression of energy and eagerness, and it allows you to control your body language.

If you rock back on your heels, you convey the impression of retreating. If you lean forward with fists clinched and lips tight, you give a threatening impression. If you lean forward with a relaxed smile, you're telling your listener, "I'm interested in you."

# WATCH YOUR POSITION

Your position relative to your audience or conversation partner also conveys messages. If you're talking to an individual and you plan a long, relaxed chat, offer your conversation partner a seat and take one yourself. Make sure the seats are side by side or facing each other at an angle. Those are friendly positions. When two people face each other directly, it suggests that they're ready to argue or do some heavy negotiating.

If you're talking to an individual and you want it to be a private conversation, point your feet directly toward the person you're talking to and maintain eye contact with that person only. That should be enough to wave off all but the nosiest intruders. If you're talking to an individual and you want to signal a third party that it's all right to join in, face your conversation partner at an angle so that imaginary lines beneath the soles of your feet will meet to form an incomplete triangle. Or stand with one foot pointing outward, away from your partner.

# HOW TO SAY GOOD-BYE

There are numerous non-verbal ways to signal an end to a conversation. If you've been sitting, simply stand up as you speak. If you're already standing, shift your position slightly, away from your partner. Little gestures also tell your partner that you're ready to break off the conversation. Glancing at your watch, straightening your tie, or adjusting your jewelry are all ways of saying, "Well, that's about it, my friend. I must be going." Touching the other person gently is a warm way of making your exit. Rubbing your hands together or brushing imaginary lint off your suit tells your partner, "This isn't a brush-off, but I really must be going."

# COMMUNICATING THROUGH SEATING

If you're talking to a group, you communicate by the seating arrangement. A circular arrangement means everyone is invited to join in. A horseshoe or T formation focuses attention on the head table or the bend of the horseshoe. Arranging seats side by side in rows facing the speaker indicates that the speaker plans to do the talking and audience participation is expected to be limited. Standing behind a podium establishes the speaker as the expert. The speaker can break the formality by stepping in front of the podium and inviting the audience to join the discussion.

# LOWER YOUR VOICE

Voice tones convey messages too. Low, well-modulated speech soothes. High-pitched, fast-paced speech irritates. Consciously control your breathing as you speak. This will regulate the pace of your speech and will help you keep your voice tone comfortably low.

# USE YOUR HANDS

Gestures come naturally to many people—especially those who have developed conversational skills. If you haven't learned to punctuate your words with gestures, begin to practice—with friends or before a mirror. Don't wait until you've made your point, then gesture. Let your gestures *accompany* your words. Don't clench your fist, shake your finger or cross your arms. Those are unfriendly gestures. Don't raise your hands above your head. That breaks eye contact.

# READING NON-VERBAL SIGNALS

With practice, you can read the non-verbal language of others. When the eyes of the person you're talking to become vacant or start scanning the room for someone else to move on to, you know your conversation is going nowhere. Folded arms also tell you that you're not turning the other person on. If this is a serious talk and you want it to continue, try recapturing attention with direct questions. The problem may be that you've been dominating the conversation and your partner hasn't had a chance to join in. Questions offer that opportunity. If you're addressing an audience and you notice your listeners crossing and recrossing legs, you know you're losing them. It's time for a dash of humor or a flourish of eloquence.

Want to know what the other person is really thinking? "Listen" to the body language. If Paula is rubbing her forefinger and thumb together, she's holding something back. If you've made your sales presentation and Joe stares at the ceiling and blinks his eyes rapidly, give him a little time. He's thinking it over. If he takes a deep breath and sighs, he's reached his decision. Find out what it is. If he says "Yes," get it on the dotted line before he changes his mind.

When you're trying to explain to Margaret the difference between transitive and intransitive verbs, she may say, "I understand." But if she rubs one eye, you might want to go over the difference one more time. Her body language is telling you she really doesn't get it.

When your supplier says he'll have those parts delivered by Friday come hell or high water, watch his feet. If they're tapping up and down, expect either high water or drastically rising temperatures, but don't look for the parts on Friday. His lips are saying "yes, yes," but his feet are saying, "I'm not so sure."

## WATCH THOSE SMILES

Most mothers know instinctively how to tell when their children are lying. There are ways of detecting untruthfulness in strangers, too. A crooked smile is often a sign of insincerity. Genuine smiles usually are symmetrical. A facial expression that lasts longer than four or five seconds is usually a phony expression. Sometimes you may see a fleeting frown followed by a broad smile. Believe the frown. The fleeting expression is the spontaneous one. What follows is usually a phony expression intended to mask the real one.

The person who looks you directly and naturally in the eye is usually more reliable than the person who avoids direct eye contact— or who forces direct eye contact.

# THE PYGMALION EXPERIMENT

Your non-verbal signals may be communicating a great deal more than you realize. The famous Pygmalion Experiment of 1964 demonstrated the profound influence of unconscious non-verbal language on others.

Teachers were given two groups of students to work with. Tests showed both groups of students to be about equal in scholastic ability. But the teachers were told that one group was bright while the other group was not so bright.

At the end of the year, guess which group had the higher achievement level. The children who were labeled "bright" had outperformed those who were labeled "not so bright."

What had happened? The teachers, through body language and other non-verbal clues, had favored the students they thought were bright. They had higher expectations of these students, and the students lived up to the expectations. They had lower expectations of the other group, and this group lived down to those expectations.

# A RED CHECK FOR LUEBIRDIE

Sarah Lewis, a colleague of mine in North Carolina, passed along a positive experience she had with non-verbal language in a class of elementary-school pupils. She had a student named Luebirdie, who was a slow learner. Sarah used a lot of ingenuity on Luebirdie, devising little math games and other special techniques to help her learn the basic skills.

When Sarah gave the class an assignment, she would usually give Luebirdie a different work sheet—one that was more appropriate to her learning level. As the students finished their work sheets, they would bring them to the teacher. Sarah would correct them with a red felt-tipped pen, then give them another task.

One day Luebirdie proudly brought her work sheet to Sarah. The child was confident that she had done well on the exercise, and indeed she had. When Sarah had finished looking over the work, she reached over and, with the felt-tipped pen, made a check mark on Luebirdie's cheek.

"What's that for, Mrs. Lewis?" asked the child.

"That's for working smart today," replied the teacher. "I'm marking you smart."

Luebirdie went back to her seat glowing with pride. The other children noticed what had happened. Soon there was a line of pupils in front of the teacher's desk, eager to submit their worksheets for approval and to receive the coveted red check marks on the cheek.

The pupils went to lunch bearing their red check marks like medals of honor. When the other students asked them about the marks, they answered: "We've been marked smart, and our teacher gave us a red check because we are smart."

The next day, Luebirdie came to school looking not quite as well-scrubbed as usual. There was a little dirt around one cheek, but the red check was still there—a little smeared, but still visible. Luebirdie would not let her mother wash the smart mark away. Through that one instinctive, non-verbal gesture, Sarah Lewis had given Luebirdie and her classmates the precious gift of self-esteem, which made them believe they were smart and act as if they were smart.

# COMMUNICATING THROUGH WORDS

Although only 7% of your communicating is done through the written or spoken word, verbal language offers us the most precise way of conveying complex ideas. Therefore, we need to pay careful attention to the way we communicate verbally.

Understanding is the key aim of all communications. You cannot lead or teach or inspire unless you achieve understanding. And understanding is best achieved when there is mutual respect between the transmitter and the receiver of communications. If you respect the people with whom you communicate, you will not try to impress them with how much you know and how little they know. You will approach them at their own level, without appearing to be condescending. You will explain things in terms with which they are familiar. When communicating face to face, you will ask for feedback, to make sure that they are receiving your message accurately. You will give them feed-back so that you can be sure you understand them correctly.

Verbal communication falls into two basic categories: written and oral. Like non-verbal communication, it involves the use of symbols: letters and punctuation marks in the case of written communication; sounds in the case of oral communication. But in verbal communication, the symbols have formalized meanings. That means that verbal language can be somewhat more precise than non-verbal language, assuming that both sender and receiver share common understandings of the symbols used. That, of course, is not always the case. No two people have precisely identical vocabularies. And the unique set of experiences each individual has acquired lends color and texture to word meanings that are distinctive to each individual. Therefore, we need to be careful in choosing our words.

## TWO-WAY AND ONE-WAY COMMUNICATION

The right choice of words is particularly important in one-way communications. In two-way communication, as when you're engaged in direct conversation with an individual, you can observe the individual's reaction, weigh the response, and judge whether your meaning has been accurately discerned. If you find that there was a misunderstanding, you can correct it on the spot.

When you're communicating through writing, or addressing a large audience, immediate two-way communication may be impractical. It is important, therefore, that you choose your words more carefully and make your points with maximum precision. If you're misunderstood, there may not be a chance to correct the misapprehension.

## BRYANT'S GHOST STORY

It took some careful two-way communication to clear up a fear that my son Bryant acquired through faulty one-way communication.

When William and Bryant were small children, Maxcy and I sometimes had to make out-of-town trips at the same time. When we did, we usually split the boys between their two sets of grandparents. William loved to go to the O'Tuels' house, where his grandmother would read to him and recite poetry to him. Bryant loved to visit the Wards, where his grandmother doted on him as "the Sugarbear." But on one occasion, Bryant balked at staying with my parents.

"Why?" I asked. "I thought you loved going to visit Grandma and Granddaddy Ward."

"I do," he said, "but I don't like to go to their church."

"Why?"

"I'm afraid of the ghost."

A little patient questioning revealed the glitch in understanding.

In my parents' fundamentalist faith, there were frequent appeals for the Holy Ghost to come down. Bryant's concept of a ghost was quite different from his grandparents' concept of the loving helper from on high. Once he understood that the Holy Ghost was really the Spirit of God, he was comfortable again at his grandparents' house.

## GRANDMA'S BIRTH-CONTROL PILLS

On the speaking circuit, one of my favorite stories involves a woman in her 80s who asked her doctor for birth-control pills.

"You don't need birth-control pills," said the doctor.

"Oh yes I do," said the octogenarian. "I sleep much better when I have them."

"My dear," explained the doctor patiently, "there is no correlation whatsoever between birth-control pills and sleeping."

"You're not listening to me," she said. "Every morning when I get up, I pour my granddaughter a cup of coffee. I pop one of those pills into her coffee, and I sleep a lot better the next night."

The woman and the doctor were on different wave lengths, but immediate two-way communications enabled her to tune him in to her meaning.

## THE EARS MAY BETRAY YOU

The spoken word can be particularly treacherous, especially when you're dealing with people who have low language skills—as with young children or poorly educated adults.

I remember the time I was in grammar school and the teacher told the class we were going on a field trip. I wasn't excited at all. A field was something I worked hard in at home, and I wasn't eager to break away from the school routine to go visit one. How was I to know that, to my citified classmates, a field trip could be something as exciting as a trip to Raleigh to see Sonja Henie ice skate?

A kindergarten youngster in Dorchester County showed how the untrained ear can distort the spoken sound. He had failed to bring an object for show-and-tell, but he had a story to tell. The story involved a "dumb ol' pitcher." The expression didn't seem to make sense in the context, so the teacher asked the little boy to draw a "dumb ol' pitcher." What he drew was a large dog. To this rural youngster, the words "Doberman Pincer" translated to "dumb ol' pitcher."

Another youngster's eyes lit up with recognition when the teacher asked who could tell her about the Declaration of Independence.

"I know what that is," he said. "My uncle had his removed."


# WORDS CAN LAND YOU IN A MESS

Words change meanings in different cultural environments. If a new family moves to town from another area and you invite them to your house for dinner, better make sure the word "dinner" means the same to them as it does to you. In some environments, dinner is the mid-day meal. The evening meal is called "supper." In others, the noon meal is called "lunch" and dinner comes some time after five. If you don't clarify your meaning, you may find your guests on your doorstep at noon when you were expecting them at six.

A Northern family moving into Horry County, South Carolina, was charmed by the friendliness and generosity of the local people. Once, when they stopped by a farm house to ask directions to Myrtle Beach, the farmer noted their accents and said, "How'd you folks like to take some good fresh corn home with you?"

The Northerners said that was very nice of him. So the farmer walked over to a truck full of freshly harvested roasting ears. He brought a dozen or so ears of sweet corn and put them in the trunk of their car.

"Is that a mess?" he asked.

"Oh, gracious no," said the lady in the family.

So the farmer went back to the truck and fetched another dozen ears.

"Is that a mess?" he asked.

"Oh no," said the woman. "That's not a mess at all."

After the farmer returned with his third dozen, the woman protested.

"This is awfully generous of you, but that's far more corn than our family can eat."

"I thought you said it wasn't a mess," said the farmer.

"Oh no, it's not a mess. You've stacked it in the trunk very neatly, but we'll never be able to eat that much corn."

The word "mess" had a different meaning to the farmer and to the Northern family. To the Northerners, it meant something untidy. To the Horry County farmer, it meant a quantity sufficient to make a single meal for the family. When a Horry County housewife says, "I fixed me up a mess of greens for supper," she doesn't mean that she did a sloppy job of cooking. She means that she prepared enough greens to make a meal for herself.

Even the word "greens" can land some people in a semantic mess. Faith Sellers discovered that many years ago when she moved from Philadelphia to the sleepy South Carolina town of Summerville. Her husband headed a bus company in nearby Charleston, and one of his associates displayed his Southern hospitality by sending home a mess of collards.

"Somebody sent you some greens," her husband told her as he walked through the door.

Now collard greens are a delicacy only the native palate can truly appreciate. In some parts of South Carolina they make collard kraut, which has a bouquet somewhere between Octagon soap and limburger cheese and which you shouldn't try unless your Carolina roots go at least as far back as the Charleston Earthquake. But the most common way to fix collards is to boil them in a pot with a thick slice of fatback or—in prosperous times—with some fragrant ham hock.

Faith, having no background whatever in Palmetto State cuisine, did with those collard greens what any civilized Philadelphian would do with any clump of greenery. She took her Lenox vase—the one she had received as a wedding gift—from the china cabinet and carefully arranged the broad-leafed greenery in it. She proudly displayed the arrangement in her parlor, watering it carefully each day.

Later, when Faith met her husband's associate, the subject of the collard greens came up.

"They were lovely," she said. "I put them in a vase on the mantel and kept them watered and I thought they never would wilt."

You should have heard them roaring at the church picnic when that story got around. Faith got the last laugh, though. She later did an arrangement of collard greens, entered them in a flower show— and won a ribbon. Many an unacclimated Yankee emigree still swears that Faith discovered the highest and best use for collard greens.


# SEMANTIC BAGGAGE

Words often carry "semantic baggage," and we have to be careful about how we use them. A white Virginia politician was accustomed to referring to his male friends as "boys," as in "good ol' boys." When he casually referred to a legislator named L. Douglas Wilder as a "boy," he kicked up a storm of controversy. Wilder, who later became governor of Virginia, is black. To blacks, the designation "boy" has long been associated with servitude, and it is considered condescending and insulting. The white politician later mended his fences and became a supporter of Wilder. But one has to be careful.

## JUST CALL IT A SPADE

Sometimes we're tempted to show off our vocabularies just to impress people. If the words you use are unknown to your partner in communication, you're communicating all right, but your message may not be what you think it is. The person on the receiving end may conclude that you're pompously and egotistically asinine and may tune you out permanently. When you have to talk about an implement for manual excavation, force yourself to call it a spade— or better yet, a shovel. Your audience—whether ignorant or erudite— will think better of you.

The use of unfamiliar words and expressions can be particularly hazardous to understanding. Even you may not know precisely what they mean. A small-town correspondent for a metropolitan daily newspaper once reported on a PTA meeting in which "many suggestive remarks were made." The correspondent thought "suggestive remarks" were the same thing as "helpful suggestions." She didn't know that a common meaning of that term is "tending to suggest something that is improper or indecent." Stick with tried and true expressions, using new ones only when you have heard them or read them enough to absorb their precise meanings.

## AVOID JARGON

Often, people in a particular profession like to impress outsiders by using professional jargon. Jargon can be a significant barrier to communication. Indulge me another story from my speaking-circuit repertoire of anecdotes.

A woman I knew in Dorchester County had a large family of children, and she loved to have them over for Sunday dinner. During the heat of summer, she would pass out fans after dinner—the kind funeral homes used to distribute. The children would sit on the front porch and fan themselves while the fried chicken, potato salad, turnip greens, banana pudding and iced tea settled in their stomachs.

Finally, the children decided it was time to go together and buy Mama an air conditioner. For Christmas, they presented her with a check and directed her to a major appliance store in Charleston.

# NO IFS ANDS OR BTUS

The salesperson was eager to impress her with his expertise in air conditioning, which meant that he also wanted to impress her with her own ignorance.

"How many BTU's were you looking for?" he asked.

"What's a BTU?" she asked.

The salesperson sighed his "here's-another-ignorant-clodhopper" sigh and explained: "The letters 'BTU' stand for British Thermal Units, and it's a commonly used measurement of cooling or heating capacity, and it's equal to about 252 calories. That's the amount of energy it takes to raise the temperature of one pound of water from 62° Fahrenheit to 63° Fahrenheit. You need to tell me your BTU requirements before I can recommend the proper air conditioner for your barn. . . . er home."

By now, Mama was into her slow burn.

"Listen, mister," she said. "I don't care about your B.T.U.'s. All I want is an air conditioner to cool my B.U.T., and it's as big as a T.U.B."

The salesperson might have simplified the transaction by asking the customer about the size of her house, the size of the space she intended to cool and the amount of insulation in the walls and ceilings.

# SHORT AND SIMPLE SENTENCES

The cautionary advice about oral communication is doubly applicable to written communications. Written language has a permanence that the spoken word doesn't always have. Therefore, it can come back to haunt you. Also, as previously noted, written language does not provide for immediate feed-back. So it's doubly important that you be precise and accurate the first time.

The best advice I can give about written communication is to keep it simple. Don't use big words, especially if they're unfamiliar to you. And don't write long, complicated sentences. Studies have shown that when your writing averages 16 words per sentence, about 90% of your readers can comprehend you. When it averages 30 words per sentence, about 90% of your readers *cannot* comprehend you. In this chapter, I have been averaging just about 13.5 words to the sentence. Some of the sentences are fairly long, but most are short. Can you understand me?

When you write short sentences, you reduce the possibility that you will forget what you want to say before you've finished saying it. Keep sentences short by expressing one idea to a sentence.

## READ WHAT YOU'VE WRITTEN

Think carefully about what you want to say. Then write it down and read it. Better yet, have somebody else read it, to see whether it makes sense. If you follow the advice in this chapter, you are unlikely to embarrass yourself by writing sentences such as these compiled by Emile and Diana Lizi from letters parents have written to teachers:

** This is to certify that Richard was needed at home for some important reason.

** I kept Mary Jo at home today because she was not feeling too bright.

** Please excuse Vickie on Monday, Tuesday and Wednesday. She had an absent tooth.

** Marcia was absent Friday because she was sick and had craps in her stomach.

** Please excuse Jim Tuesday. He had loose vowels.

** Please excuse Robert for being absent January 28, 29, 30, 31, 32, and 33.

** Please excuse Katrina for being absent. She was sick and I had her shot.

** Please excuse Sandy from gym today. She is administrating.

** My son James is under the doctor's care and should not take PE classes. Please execute him.

** Please excuse Mike's absence for he has a cough and a cold which comes and goes. Yesterday it came.

** Shirley was absent yesterday as she was nauseating.

** Ben is at home for a few more days yet. He is carrying a case of measles.

** Lois has got a little bit of the trots, so please let her go when she wants.

## EMULATE GOOD WRITERS AND SPEAKERS

One of the best ways to learn how to express yourself clearly is to read good writing, listen to effective speakers, and use your dictionary. When you read and listen to effective communicators, their language patterns become established in your subconscious. You will subconsciously begin to emulate their patterns. The result will be better, clearer communication. With the ability to communicate, you will have acquired a key success skill for the 1990s and beyond.

# Chapter Seven

# *Become a Professional*

*Between the amateur and the professional . . . there is a difference not only in degree but in kind. The skillful man is, within the function of his skill, a different integration, a different nervous and muscular and psychological organization.*

*—BERNARD DE VOTO*

Professionals don't wait around to be discovered. They discover themselves. They don't wait until responsibility is offered. They assume responsibility. They don't wait to be selected as leaders. They select themselves. Professionals don't push; they lead. When you're a professional, people come to you to find out how it's done. And when you've done your thing, it always has that finished, polished look, whether your "thing" is driving a golf ball, teaching an English class, selling shoes or wiring a breaker box.

# PROFESSIONALISM IS HOW YOU DO IT

To achieve prosperity, you need to become a professional at what you do.

We often think of professionals as being doctors, lawyers, engineers and other highly educated types. But professional, as we will use the term, applies less to what you do than it does to how you do it. Professionals are people who believe in putting the last full measure of quality into everything they do.

Professionals master the skills of their vocations and constantly look for opportunities to improve them. They are not content to do things the "right way." They are always looking to do things a better way.

Professionals know their businesses thoroughly. They keep up with the latest developments and are always ready to put new knowledge into practice.

Professionals exude confidence. When you're a professional, people come to you to find out how it's done. And when you've done your thing, it always has that finished, polished look, whether your "thing" is driving a golf ball, teaching an English class, selling shoes or wiring a breaker box.

It's always a pleasure to see a real pro at work. We often underestimate the professional qualities of people we know only in a social context. The wife of a real-estate agent once remarked, "I never really knew how good Richard was at his job until we went into the market for our own home. Then I saw him in action as a negotiator. He was really good!"

Professionals are perceived as good because they always try to give their work that something extra that sets it apart from non-professional work.

James F. Byrnes, who served as a United States Senator, Supreme Court justice, assistant to the president of the United States, secretary of State and governor of South Carolina, was describing the professional's attitude when he passed along this wisdom to a young scholar named Jim Mahaffey:

I discovered at an early age that the difference between an individual being "average" and "tops" is explained in three simple words: *"and then some."*

Top people do what is expected of them—*and then some.*

They are thoughtful of others—*and then some.*

They are considerate and kind—*and then some.*

They meet their obligations and responsibilities fairly and equally—*and then some.*

They are good friends to their friends—*and then some.*

They can be counted on in an emergency—*and then some.*

## FIND YOUR TALENT AND REFINE IT

If you want to become a professional, find a field that will enable you to go full speed ahead without departing from your behavior style. Find something that will enable you to use your highest abilities. Then become as good at it as you possibly can.

Take advantage of every opportunity to learn. If it requires a college degree, obtain that degree. It will be worth the time, effort and expense you put into it. Be alert for lectures, seminars and workshops that will add to your inventory of knowledge and skills. Find someone who is already an accomplished pro and ask for counsel and guidance. That individual probably will be flattered by the request and will be eager to become your mentor.

## ACQUIRE PERSONAL POWER

The most important thing you can acquire en route to becoming a professional is personal power. Personal power does not depend upon your position in an organization. Lee Iacocca was president of Ford Motor Company one day, relegated to an out-of-the-way office the next. But Iacocca's personal power carried him through the crisis, and his demotion at Ford actually set the stage for greater national prominence.

Personal power doesn't depend strictly upon knowledge. You may have a head full of knowledge today, but it can become obsolete by tomorrow.

Personal power depends upon your ability to influence people in positive ways. You influence people by making them feel good about doing the things you want them to do. If you are pleasant and cheerful toward others, they will like you and want to please you. If you make them feel important, they will help you enhance your own importance. If you demonstrate honesty and good character, they will trust you, and the trust of others is an important source of power. If you respect them, they will respect you, and that respect will lead them to value your opinion and your goals.

Professionals think of themselves as problem-solvers, not problem finders or problem-creators. When presented with difficult tasks, they don't give you reasons for not doing the job; they look for ways to get it done.

# THE SIX QUALITIES OF PERSONAL POWER

** Positive attitude. Professionals are can-do people, which means they are optimists. They learn to keep their self-esteem up through positive self-talk. We all talk to ourselves, either mentally or out loud. Studies indicate that 80% of the self-talk we do is negative. Turn that percentage around. Keep using positive affirmations: "I like myself." "I am confident." "I can do what I want to do."

** Willingness to take risks. There is no progress without change, and no change without risk. People with personal power go into risks with heads-up attitudes. Ask yourself: "What is the worst thing that could happen?" Once you assess the worst, it usually isn't as bad as you feared. Then ask: "What is likely to happen?" This gives you a realistic basis for determining whether the risk is worth taking. Finally ask, "What is the best that could happen." If you determine that the probable outcome is worth the risk, go for it, and expect the best.

** Willingness to set goals. Goals keep you focused on what you want to accomplish. They give you direction. By setting goals, you can actually create your future. Walt Disney started his trek to fame and fortune by drawing a mouse. The mouse would have been no more than idle doodling had Disney not imbued it with a vision and a goal. Now millions of people annually visit Disney World and Disneyland, watch Disney movies and read Disney comics. And the whole empire began with a drawing of a mouse that eventually was named Mickey.

** Willingness to take the initiative. This is going to be an increasingly valuable asset in the future. In rapidly changing circumstances, the winner will be the person who is able to get a jump on the ball. And the future is going to bring rapidly changing circumstances. The old bureaucratic motto, "Don't just do something; stand there!" was never good policy. If you stand there, you're likely to be standing alone—or at least in the company of a pack of losers. The go-getters will have gone off and left you. So if you have a love affair with the status quo, break it off. Be constantly looking for action you can take to make what you're doing a little better.

** Ability to empower others. President George Bush decided to evict Saddam Hussein from Kuwait, but he couldn't do it alone. So he empowered Secretary of

Defense Richard Cheney to get the job done. Did Cheney hog the glory? He went to Colin Powell, chairman of the Joint Chiefs of Staff. Powell turned the job over to General Norman Schwartzkopf. Schwartzkopf had wide strategic latitude, but he couldn't oust the Iraqi Republican Guard alone. He empowered his Air Force and Navy colleagues to carry the war to the enemy and finally unleashed his field commanders, who led their troops to victory. At each stage of the operation, the man in charge multiplied his power by empowering others. That's the key to succeeding in the business and professional world. Empower your subordinates; give them responsibility; praise their achievements; share with them the fruits of success. The more you empower them, the more they'll empower you.

** Project power. Dress, speak and carry yourself as if you were in charge and expected others to recognize you as a person of authority. Slouched shoulders project weakness. Hands clasped in front or behind you project weakness. You don't project authority by twirling your hair, fingering your jewelry, stroking your moustache, biting your nails, or jingling the coins in your pockets. Stand or sit straight. Keep your hands below your shoulders. Keep your feet apart—so that the span between the outsides of your shoes is about the same as the span of your shoulders. Speak clearly. And listen a lot.

# TEN HIGH-PERFORMANCE TRAITS

Dr. Charles A. Garfield, a leading authority on people performance, has a similar list of qualities characteristic of high-performing leaders:

** They exhibit foresight and the ability to plan strate-
   gically. Thus they are less consumed by short-term gain
   at the expense of long-term planning.

** They decide in advance what people and other resources
   they will need to complete a project.

** They refuse to become entrapped at any level of performance; they're always reaching higher.

** They have a superior ability to take creative risks; they
   don't withdraw into "comfort zones."

** They exhibit extremely high levels of self-confidence
   and self-worth.

** They have a significant need for responsibility and control.

** They mentally rehearse key situations.

** Their missions matter to them and they approach them
   with a great deal of enthusiasm.

** They concentrate on solving problems rather than on
   fixing blame.

** They tend to assume ownership of their ideas and
   products.[1]

Dr. Garfield makes it clear that, while some people seem naturally
to possess such leadership traits, others can, and often do, cultivate
them.

Being a professional means much more than acquiring a skill.
It means reflecting certain high standards in every aspect of life.

---

[1] Charles A. Garfield, Ph.D., *Peak Performance,* (Tarcher/Houghton
Mifflin, 1984).

# LOOK LIKE A PROFESSIONAL

Your appearance goes a long way toward establishing you as a professional. Not all professionals wear pin-stripe suits on the job. If you're a professional painter, that might be a totally inappropriate outfit. But professionals are careful about their visual images. Dirty, frayed and ill-fitting uniforms do not inspire confidence in your professional ability, whether you wear the dress blues of an Air Force general or the starched whites of a registered nurse.

If your job does require men to wear suits and ties and women to wear heels and hose, then fashions become a major concern for you. It is important that you dress for success.

Some people have a natural eye for coordinating colors. Some people know instinctively what styles flatter them and what styles make them look skinny or dumpy, stuffy or flaky.

If you are not blessed with this intuitive gift, take advantage of those who are. There are fashion magazines on the book stands and fashion sections in the newspapers. Read them for hints on dressing for success. Department stores have fashion consultants. Use them. Observe the dress habits of someone of your age and build who has achieved success in your field and who looks the part. Find a friend who is knowledgeable about colors and styles and invite him or her to go shopping with you. It doesn't have to be someone of your gender. Many men who are indifferent about clothing styles dress like fashion plates because their wives know how to choose their clothes. I can even name one woman whose husband chooses her outfits—and does an outstanding job.

Do not regard fashion as a frivolous avocation. It's serious business in the corporate world. The professional is looked upon as a representative of the firm, and how the professional dresses reflects favorably or unfavorably upon the firm. It can even affect the bottom line. Suppose you lose a major contract for your company because your dress and demeanor kept you from gaining the confidence of the decision-maker with whom you were negotiating.

As we have seen, the way you look sends a powerful message to the people with whom you deal. How can you communicate effectively through the spoken word if your listener is distracted by the clashing colors or freakish lines of your outfit?

Even the most impeccably dressed person will appear unprofessional if the appearance is not finished off with good grooming. A three-day growth of beard may not have held back Yassir Arafat or Tom Selleck, but not many people achieve success through guerrilla organizations or television roles. Most people look for clean-shaven faces or neat beards on the male professionals they patronize. Extreme hair-dos and outlandish jewelry make women look non-professional. And even the most expensively tailored suits and dresses need to be cleaned and pressed regularly. Shoes need to be shined and missing buttons need to be replaced. A true professional must look the part.

Needless to say, a professional must also smell the part. This not only calls for regular bathing (that goes without saying) but also discretion in one's choice of perfumes and colognes. One's fragrance should be a subtle whisper, not an insistent shout.

## TALK LIKE A PROFESSIONAL

A professional speaks in a strong, clear voice. Not a booming voice that drowns out every other voice around, but a calm, firm voice that says, "I don't have to shout for attention."

During the presidential campaign of 1988, George Bush reportedly engaged a voice coach, who counseled him to lower his voice a little to project a more commanding image. Jimmy Carter's high, piping voice undoubtedly made it more difficult for him to capture the attention and the imagination of the nation. Ronald Reagan's voice was soothingly rich. Listen to the voices of Winston Churchill and Franklin D. Roosevelt—two of the more charismatic leaders of the 20th century. Their voices projected confidence and authority.

Shrill voices make people nervous. Low, calm voices inspire confidence.

But having a good voice serves no useful purpose unless you have something to say.

Professional people are knowledgeable people, and they have something to say. As a professional, vocalize your commitment to excellence. Make it clear to everyone that you adhere to high standards and expect others to do the same. Talk about the things you believe in.

Learn to speak clearly, forcefully and grammatically. During the great Depression, Dizzy Dean, the ace pitcher for the Saint Louis Cardinals, was once reproached because he repeatedly used the word "ain't."

"Lots of people who ain't sayin' *ain't* ain't eatin,' " scoffed Dean.

If your pitching arm is of Hall of Fame quality, don't worry about grammar. Otherwise, don't pay any attention to Dizzy Dean's pronouncements. Sure, he made it as a sportscaster, but the world of sportscasting has room for only one Dizzy Dean per generation.

The professional, in whatever field, should learn to use good grammar and to speak clearly and succinctly. Tape yourself in normal conversation. How often do you say "you know," or "I mean," or "and stuff like that"? Stuff like that is the earmark of the non-professional.

The professional also avoids faddish expressions such as "I'm like" or "I go" as words of attribution. Try to picture this conversation between a CEO and his vice president for development:

**CEO:** How are we doing on that new line of widgets?

**VP:** I just talked to Joe down in testing, and he goes like they're being held up by problems in the O-rings and stuff like that.

**CEO:** Can't you light a fire under them? If we don't get this product on the market, the competition's going to get there first.

**VP:** I know, chief, I've, you know, been telling him stuff like that. I'm like, "Amalgamated Gizmos is, you know, looking into the same thing," and he goes, "If them O-rings don't hold, the lubricant and stuff will leak out, y'know what I mean, and then the bearings will overheat and the whole widget will, you know, fly apart or whatever. And I'm like, well, you know, do your best to speed things up, and stuff like that, you know. And he goes . . ."

Actually, the VP may be the next thing to go and he'll be like unemployed. Top leaders look for professionals who sound professional when they're talking to others about their company or its products.

Whatever you say, get to the point. A professional's time is valuable. And especially when you're talking to a High D, it's important that you state the facts clearly, simply and concisely.

## LISTEN LIKE A PROFESSIONAL

You learn a lot more when you're listening than you do when you're talking. Professionals know that, and they take the time to hear what others have to say. Listening is a good way to pick up information and to acquire new ideas.

There's an art to listening. Some people listen just long enough to get a general idea of what the speaker is saying. Then they tune out the speaker and start framing their responses. In so doing, they often miss the speaker's point or misconstrue what was said. The professional way is to pay close attention to what is being said. Look for things you can learn from the speaker's words. Make mental or written notes of the points being made. This can help you frame a response *after* the speaker has finished. If there's something you don't understand, ask for repetition or clarification. This will let the speaker know that you're listening and that you're interested in what you're hearing.

Don't step on the speaker's lines. Make your response only after the speaker has finished talking. You'll have plenty of time to say what you want to say.

The salesperson who listens to customers and prospects will pick up a great deal of useful information. What is it that customers like or dislike about the product? What can be done to improve it from the customer's standpoint? What competitors have been calling on this customer or prospect? What is the competition offering? What does the customer or prospect like or dislike about the competition's products?

I'm reminded of the dog-food manufacturer that marketed a new product line. The dog food had been scientifically formulated to provide the ultimate in canine nutrition. The packaging had been carefully designed to catch the eye of the dog-owner. The advertising campaign had been carefully planned and executed so that dog-owners everywhere knew about the product. Everything had been done to give the new dog food a successful launching.

But something wasn't going right. Customers seemed to go for the introductory offer, but they weren't coming back for more. The company's executives called in advertising and marketing consultants. Their advertising and marketing campaign had been textbook perfect. They checked back over their nutritional formulas. All the ingredients were there to turn Fido into Supermutt. So why weren't the customers coming back?

A salesperson for the dog food company was putting the question to the manager of a grocery store that had stocked the product.

"Ask him," said the manager, pointing to a shopper who was browsing in the pet-food aisle. "He bought one bag of your product, but hasn't bought one since."

"Sir," said the salesperson politely, "I notice that you're shopping for dog food. Have you ever tried our new brand, "Doggie Delight"?

*142*

"Yep," said the customer.

"Do you plan to buy it again?"

"Nope," came the reply.

"Could you tell me why you don't plan to buy any more?" asked the salesperson.

"My dog didn't like it."

A little listening on the salesperson's part accomplished more than all the Monday-morning quarterbacking by the experts.

Listening pays off, too, when you're a supervisor of people. Ford Motor Company isn't the only company that has discovered the value of listening to what production workers have to say. In other companies where employees were treated with professional respect, the workers have given management an abundance of ideas that could be taken to the bank.

Pat Carrigan has often been cited as one of the most successful plant managers in the General Motors organization. She is a former third-grade school teacher. One of her insights into management is that people perform better when they are happy. She set about making her employees happy. One of her techniques was to listen. Carrigan would remove all the office doors, making management fully accessible to employees. But she didn't wait for them to come to her. She spent a large portion of her time talking to employees, getting to know them, and asking them for ideas.

## ACT LIKE A PROFESSIONAL

You've seen those signs on the backs of big trucks: "The driver of this vehicle is a professional. If you see this vehicle being operated in an unsafe manner, please call——."

You know what to expect of a professional driver: professional courtesy. The professional driver pulls over to give you that little extra margin of safety when you're passing. The professional driver signals you when it's safe to pull back into the right lane. The professional driver doesn't try to intimidate you by tailgating. The professional driver pulls into the left lane, where feasible, to give you an opportunity to merge safely from the entry ramp into the traffic lanes.

Professional drivers thereby observe the same standards as professionals in other lines of work. They are considerate. They treat people with kindness, *and then some.*

When a server in a nice restaurant is gruff and unaccommodating, we say, "That was not professional conduct." When the CEO of a Fortune 500 corporation publicly humiliates a subordinate, we say, "That was not professional." No matter how lofty or how humble the title, we expect professionals to meet certain standards.

Victor Kiam, the man who liked Remington shavers so much that he bought the company, showed professional concern for his employees. Once while a television crew was filming a program on the company, Kiam excused himself for a moment and, off camera, walked over to ask a worker about her sick husband. The CEO told the worker to lean on the company; that it would stand behind her in her difficulty.

The woman later told a television crewmember: "I would follow Mr. Kiam to the ends of the earth and work my fingers to the bone for him."

Fill your work force with people like her, and look out, Japan!

Professionals also know how to be flexible under stress. The world is yours, wrote Rudyard Kipling:

> If you can keep your head
> When all about you
> Are losing theirs
> And blaming it on you;
> If you can trust yourself
> When all men doubt you,
> And make allowance
> For their doubting too. . . .

144

That's flexibility.

Acting like a professional means making things happen. It means taking one step every day to make your organization better. That doesn't mean going from neighborhood business to the Fortune 500 overnight. Remember, in football most touchdowns aren't made on the kickoff. They're earned by grinding out yards that lead to first downs that lead to the scoring play. Or, as the folks in Columbus County might put it, "A yard is hard, but an inch is a cinch." Aim at being 1% better at 100 things and see what happens.

# TAKE CHARGE LIKE A PROFESSIONAL

Professionals don't wait around to be discovered. They discover themselves. They don't wait until responsibility is offered. They assume responsibility. They don't wait to be selected as leaders. They select themselves.

Does that sound like a pushy person?

Then you have the wrong perspective. Professionals don't push; they lead. There's a big difference. I've heard the story about two pastoral countries whose economies were based on sheep herding. One was quite prosperous. The other was barely making it. The difference was in the way the sheep were herded.

In the country that prospered, the shepherd led the sheep to pasture. By walking ahead, he showed the sheep the way to go. The sheep, confident in their shepherd, followed. But they felt free to leave the herd temporarily in search of an especially tempting morsel of grass or to grab a quick drink when thirsty. Because they were not pressured, they were relaxed. They grew healthy and yielded a bumper crop of fleece and a bumper crop of lambs.

In the country that languished, the shepherd drove the sheep to pasture. With no one to lead them, the sheep ventured blindly toward the grazing grounds. When one broke out of the bunch, the shepherd quickly prodded it back into the herd. No independent searches for tasty clumps. No stopping for a drink of water, except at the time and place appointed by the shepherd. The sheep were high-strung and unhappy. Their fleece was of low quality and low yield. Their lambs were few and puny.

Professionals lead by example. You can appoint yourself to a leadership role by teaching yourself that you can do it. Be the presenter and not the receiver. Look for ways to create quality and take the lead in the creation. Believe in yourself and you will find that your confidence has not been misplaced.

# BE RESPONSIBLE LIKE A PROFESSIONAL

Professionals do not run from responsibility. When there's a job to be done, they take the responsibility for doing it.

This applies whether it's a project that will lead the company toward greater profitability or a service that will result in a better community.

If you want to be a professional, increase your visibility in your work place and in your community. When your contribution can help a cause, say "yes" as often as possible.

As a professional, you'll identify with your company or your organization as a whole, and not with your own little niche within the organization. When you learn something that might be helpful to someone else in your organization, don't hoard the information just because it doesn't concern you personally. Share it, for the good of the organization. If the individual with whom you share it prospers as a result, be happy. That individual's prosperity will contribute to your organization's prosperity. And you can be confident that when the individual learns something that might benefit you, you'll hear about it.

Responsible professionals deliver on their promises. If you promise a client the job will be done by next Friday and you find you'll have to pay your employees overtime to meet the deadline and the overtime will eat up your profits, pay the overtime and meet the deadline. When your clients, customers or corporate superiors learn that your word is your bond, even when it hurts, they will invest their confidence in you. And in the long run, you'll make a healthy net profit.

## PROFESSIONALS AND MENTORS

Professional people know that they can't learn everything on their own. They need mentors and they seek out mentors. Experience is a great teacher, but experience is even more valuable when it is gained at the feet of a master.

Once you have attained mastery, it's your obligation to return the favor. Find someone who can benefit from your mentoring. You received freely; give freely.

## CULTIVATE THE CLASS OF A PROFESSIONAL

Professionals cultivate class. Their work has the stamp and the aura of class. What is class? Here's how one writer describes it:

** Class never runs scared. It is being sure-footed and confident in the knowledge that you can meet life head-on and handle whatever comes along.

** Class never makes excuses. It takes its lumps and learns from past mistakes.

** Class is considerate of others. It knows that good manners is nothing more than a series of petty sacrifices.

*147*

** Class never tries to build itself up by tearing others down. Class is *already* up, and need not strive to look better by making others look worse.

** Class can talk with crowds and keep its virtue, or walk with kings and keep the common touch. Class makes others comfortable with those who possess it because its possessors are comfortable with themselves.

** Class bespeaks an aristocracy that has nothing to do with ancestors or money. The most affluent blueblood can be totally without class while the descendant of a Welsh miner may ooze class from every pore.

Back in Columbus County, they're still talking about the encounter between Horace Hawkins and the blueblood from "up North."

If there is such a thing as a professional country storekeeper, Horace was it. He had a custom of leaving each customer with a little Bible verse. When a little girl came in to buy candy, he would say, as he handed her the change, "Suffer the little children and forbid them not to come unto me, for to such belongeth the Kingdom of Heaven."

When a young boy came in to buy an anniversary gift for his parents, Horace would say, "Honor thy father and thy mother, which is the first commandment with a promise."

The daily checker game in the back of the store was well under way when the blueblood drove up in a huge luxury sedan with an expensive horse trailer in tow.

"I need to buy a blanket for my horse," said Mr. Blueblood, glancing with obvious contempt toward the men at the checkerboard.

Horace brought back a yellow plaid blanket.

"How much is it?" asked the blueblood.

"Twenty-five dollars," said Horace.

"That's not good enough for my horse," sneered the customer. "What else do you have?"

Horace went to the back of the store and took a second blanket from the shelf—identical to the first except that it was green instead of yellow.

"How much is it?"

"That'll be $75," said Horace.

"Well, it's not good enough for my horse. Have you got anything else?"

Horace brought back a third blanket, identical to the first two except that it was red.

"This is my $250 blanket," said Horace. "Don't sell many of these around here."

The blueblood looked it over.

"I'll take it," he said, haughtily handing Horace three $100 bills.

Horace glanced at the checker players out of the corner of his eye as he handed Mr. Blueblood his change.

"He was a stranger and I took him in," he said.

The checker players held their laughter until the blueblood was out the door.

Mr. Blueblood had the wealth, but Horace had the class. And Horace was no pauper either.

If you have class, you don't need much of anything else. If you don't have it, no matter what else you have, it doesn't make much difference: You will never achieve that level of excellence that marks you as a professional.

# Chapter Eight

# *Make a Difference by 'Losing' Yourself*

---

*He that findeth his life shall lose it: and he that loseth his life for my sake shall find it.*
                              *—MATTHEW 10:39*

*When you cease to make a contribution you begin to die.*
                    *—ELEANOR ROOSEVELT*

In the work place of the future, supervisors at lower levels will be vested with more responsibility and their opinions will carry more weight. That means that the successful people of the future must be attuned not just to their individual jobs, but to the total corporate mission. Being thus attuned requires that we practice a measure of selflessness, but in the long run, selflessness is a paying investment. True greatness is achieved only by those who are willing to lose themselves in causes greater than they are.

# MAKING A DIFFERENCE

The subtle glow of dawn fringed the seaward horizon with pink. The breakers rolled to the shore, then spread themselves thin over the beach sand. As they receded, the wet sand glistened with the faint promise of daylight.

An old man walked slowly down the beach, treading the upper limits of the wave line, where the damp-packed sand offered firm footing. The glow on the horizon reminded him of summer roses long faded. The salt air reminded him that life still has a savor. The scattering of life forms on the strand reminded him of impending death.

The old man surveyed the scene sadly. The life forms were starfish, mindless creatures of the animal kingdom, fragments of life tossed up by the sea overnight, awaiting death by scorching when the sun rose high and turned hostile. Their only salvation lay in a return to the comfort of the sea. But starfish cannot move on land. Once they're beached, they lie motionless, awaiting sure death.

The old man stooped and picked up a starfish. He sailed it like a boomerang, over the shoulder of the surfline, where the water was deep and the primitive animal would have a fresh chance at life.

Then he picked up another and another, sailing the starfish back to their homes before the killer sun could accomplish its carnage.

A young jogger approached. When he discerned the old man's mission, he paused and jogged in place for a moment.

"You're wasting your time, old man," he said. "There's 30 miles of beach here, and every mile is littered with thousands of those starfish. You can't save them all, so what difference does it make?"

The old man bent over, picked up another starfish, and sent it sailing home to Mother Ocean.

"I'll bet I made a difference with that one," he said.

# THE LARGER CAUSE

To the young jogger, the old man's efforts looked futile and foolish. What's one more dead starfish in a world that has witnessed the cycle of life and death ever since the gates closed on the Garden of Eden?

The old man, though, had a reverence for life. He knew that the human life span is only a moment in eternity, but it is a precious moment. If the consequences of our existence are no more longlasting than our own time upon the earth, then our lives are futile, inconsequential drops lost in the fathomless sea of time. Those who make a difference are those who seek causes larger than they are and lose themselves in those causes. By thus "losing" their lives, such people find them.

The old man was engrossed in a cause larger than he. The saving of a few starfish would not put food on his table, would not pay the landlord, and would not pay for his Medicare supplement. But each starfish he saved meant the salvation of generations of starfish offspring. And who knows? One of the starfish rescued from the hostile beach might become the progenitor of the starfish that survive pollution, global warming or ecological disasters yet to be conceived; that assure the continuation of the starfish race so that future generations of humans might walk the beaches and enjoy the company of starfish.

By that time, surely, the old man will have long since been gathered with his forefathers, asleep in the earth that produced him. But his good deed will have lived on.

The old man was attuned not just to his own little niche in nature, but to the entire web of life. He was not an isolated creature, but a part of the universe of life. He was a tiny part, but he was able to exert influence on the whole.

# THE PERSPECTIVE OF THE WHOLE

What does an old man throwing starfish into the ocean have to do with you and the path to prosperity?

In the work place, the community, and the world of the future, successful people will be those who see themselves not as isolated individuals but as constituents of something larger. Each person must adopt the perspective of the whole and not be content with the narrow view of the part. Each person must realize that what affects the whole affects the individual units.

Charles E. Wilson, the president of General Motors whom President Eisenhower chose as his Secretary of Defense, was lampooned for saying, "What is good for the country is good for General Motors, and what is good for General Motors is good for the country."

But Wilson was not just engaging in corporate chauvinism. He made a valid point. General Motors is a giant of a corporation providing employment to hundreds of thousands of people, either directly or through its suppliers. Its prosperity has an important bearing on the prosperity of America. But without a strong domestic economy behind it, without the free marketplace guaranteed by the American system, and without the stable environment guaranteed by the American government, General Motors could not exist. The welfare of General Motors was, and is, inextricably bound to the welfare of a larger whole: the United States itself.

As an individual in a corporate work place, your welfare too is tied tightly to the welfare of a larger whole. If the corporation prospers, it can offer you better wages, better benefit packages and better job security. If it fails to prosper, your individual interests will suffer. If the corporation becomes known for quality products or excellent services, you can share the pride in the image. If its image is shoddy, you'll share the shame.

*154*

When corporations were machines and individual workers were simply interchangeable parts, no one expected the individual to take responsibility for the well-being of the corporation. That was for the CEO and a small circle of top management to worry about. Individuals who offered suggestions outside their narrow bailiwicks were told to mind their own business.

"The old system thought of the worker as a single-purpose machine tool," said Ford CEO Donald Petersen. At Ford, they still tell the story of the worker whose job was to lift heavy transmissions. One day he stopped his boss and said, "I think I know how to improve this operation."

"Forget it," snarled the boss. "We don't pay you to think."[2]

## A WELDER WHO THOUGHT

Carl Houston wasn't paid to think either, but he thought anyway. His company spurned his thinking, and paid a high price in money and prestige. Houston lost his job, but because he became involved in a cause larger than himself, more than a million people now enjoy a greater margin of safety than they might have enjoyed otherwise.

Houston was a welder from Johnson City, Tennessee. During the early '70s, he held a job supervising other welders during the construction of a nuclear power plant in Virginia. Had he taken the Performax Personal Profile System, he probably would have been identified as a High C perfectionist. He insisted that things be done properly.

Houston was involved with the welding on the reactor cooling system at the plant. This system is very critical to the safety of the reactor, for if it does not deliver the cooling water, the reactor will overheat, melt its way out of its container and spread ecological

---

[2] Robert H. Waterman Jr., *Adhocracy: The Power to Change* (Knoxville, Tennessee: Whittle Direct Books, 1990) p. 9.

disaster far and wide. The disaster at Chernobyl in the Soviet Union was the result of a partial melt-down.

The water to cool the reactor must flow through stainless steel pipes. The welds in these pipes must be performed with just the right metal at just the right temperatures. Otherwise, they may be vulnerable to corrosion.

As Houston observed the welding in the core cooling system, he noticed that some of the welds were not performed at the specified temperature. Furthermore, the welders were keeping inadequate records of the types of metal they used in the welds. Nobody could say for certain how safe they were.

Houston called this to the attention of his superiors, who minimized the problem. Even if the welding temperatures were a bit off, or the alloy used was the wrong mixture of metals, those joints were unlikely to fail during operation. And even if they did, there were back-up systems designed to get cooling water quickly to the reactor.


## WHAT DIFFERENCE DID IT MAKE?

Houston might have let the matter drop there. After all, he had discharged his responsibility. If the welds gave way at some time in the future, nobody could blame him. Furthermore, he wouldn't suffer the consequences. More than a million people would live in the shadow of that plant, but Carl Houston would not be among them. He was not a permanent resident of the area. He would be there only for the duration of the construction. Once the power plant went into operation, he would be safely at home, 500 miles away. If the system failed, it would happen years in the future, perhaps beyond his own lifetime.

But Houston saw a cause that was bigger than he was. He made his concerns known to the responsible federal agency. He talked to newspaper and television reporters. He made a nuisance of himself until a state official took up the cause. A federal hearing was conducted. As a result of his efforts, the welds were audited. Many were redone, at considerable cost to the company. Even so, the federal agency required that the welds be inspected with stepped-up frequency after the plant had gone into operation. The company might have saved itself considerable money and headaches had it listened to Houston at the outset.

Some 20 years later, the plant was operating safely. Did Carl Houston make a difference? No one can swear that the plant would have blown had the old welds been allowed to stand. But who would want to undo the safety precautions to find out?

"Why should you bother," someone might have asked Houston. "What difference does it make."

To which Houston might have replied: "I made a difference with this one."

## LEARNING TO BE SELFLESS

Houston was ahead of his time. Back in the late '60s and early '70s, people at his level of supervision were not expected to think beyond their immediate jobs. They were not expected to look at the larger picture. It was Houston's job to see that the welds were done. It was somebody else's job to worry about the chemical content of the metal and the temperature of the welds. It was somebody else's job to decide what was an acceptable risk for the million or more people whose lives might be jeopardized.

In the work place of the future, supervisors at Houston's level will be vested with more responsibility and their opinions will carry more weight. That means that the successful people of the future must be attuned not just to their individual jobs, but to the total corporate mission.

Being thus attuned requires that we practice a measure of selflessness, just as the old man practiced selflessness when he threw the

*157*

starfish back into the ocean; just as Carl Houston practiced selflessness when he put his job on the line rather than countenance those substandard welds in the reactor-cooling system.

But in the long run, selflessness is a paying investment. True greatness is achieved only by those who are willing to lose themselves in causes greater than they are.

## CINCINNATUS SAVES ROME

Such a man was Quinctus Cincinnatus, a citizen farmer in the Roman republic of the 5th century B.C. Cincinnatus wanted no more out of life than the modest pleasures of a successful small farmer. But a larger cause beckoned. Rome became involved in a battle for its life against enemy armies. The Roman army was surrounded and the Republic was on the brink of doom.

Cincinnatus put aside his plow and accepted the call to assume the office of dictator. He led Rome to victory and assured the survival of the republic. Having accomplished his purpose, he voluntarily gave up the office and went back to his farm.

## ANOTHER CITIZEN SOLDIER

The story will have a familiar ring to students of American history. During the 1770s, when freedom hung in the balance on the American continent, a gentleman farmer accepted the leadership of the Continental Army. He led it to victory and had the chance to cash in on his countrymen's esteem by claiming a sovereign's crown. Instead, he retired to his farm and quietly advocated a government in which the people were sovereign. When a powerful new office was created, he reluctantly left his farm to accept the responsibility of office. After eight years as president, George Washington voluntarily stepped down, and thereby established the two-term precedent that has been broken by only one of his successors, and was eventually codified into a constitutional amendment.

Someone might have said to Cincinnatus: "What's the difference? Rome is just an upstart political state; what difference will it make if one more petty empire bites the dust? You can do your farming regardless of who rules the Italian peninsula." But thanks to Cincinnatus, Rome had a chance to grow to something far greater than a petty empire. Had he not left his farm, Western humanity might have missed out on the enormous civilizing influence of Rome.

Someone might have said to Washington, "What's the difference? British America is just a collection of backwoods settlements. It can't matter greatly whether they're ruled by a Parliament in London or a Congress in America. You've got your farm. Enjoy it." But had Washington not left Mount Vernon, American independence might have been delayed or thwarted entirely, or the infant republic might have relapsed into monarchy or dictatorship. Without the might of a free America, who would have stopped Kaiser Wilhelm? Who would have withstood the combined forces of Hitler, Mussolini and Tojo? How would the free-enterprise system have fared against communism?

# WRITING FOR FREEDOM

Had Harriet Beecher Stowe's principal aim been to make money by writing books, she might be but a dim memory in literary circles. But she lost herself in the larger cause of freeing the American slaves of the 19th century. Her zeal for this cause led to *Uncle Tom's Cabin*, which fanned anti-slavery sentiment in Northern states and helped set the stage for the War Between the States.

# A HOSPITAL IN AFRICA

Albert Schweitzer won the Nobel Prize by losing himself in a cause larger than himself. He could have lived comfortably on his income as a theologian, philosopher, musician and physician, enjoying the pleasant life of a wealthy German before the tragedies of the World Wars. He achieved greatness, though, by involving himself in the larger community of mankind. He saw the need for a medical facility in West Africa, although he knew that the impoverished people of the region could not make it profitable. So he invested his own funds. After World War I, he rebuilt the hospital and added a leper colony.

Africa remains an impoverished, disease-ridden continent. Did Schweitzer make a difference?

He did to those individuals who sought and received help at his hospital.

# A LARGE CAUSE, A LARGE FORTUNE

Losing yourself in a larger cause doesn't mean that you have to impoverish yourself. Cincinnatus was able to retire to the comfort of his farm. Washington lived out his last days as a gentleman farmer at Mount Vernon. Schweitzer maintained a comfortable income from his medical practice, his music, his lectures and his books.

And then there was Henry Ford. Ford made his fortune by losing himself in a larger cause. He saw his mission not just as the designing and marketing of an automobile but as the empowerment of the common man.

Had Ford been content to design and sell a horseless carriage, the Ford automobile might have taken its place in history alongside the Reo, the Winton, the Pierce Arrow and the Hupmobile. But Ford's vision was larger. By building his car on an assembly line, using interchangeable parts, he was able to achieve volume production and thus make the car affordable for the average American. He could do this even while paying his workers a minimum of $5 a day—unheard of in his time. With that kind of income, the workers could afford to buy the cars they were building.

In the process of putting America on wheels and providing his workers with decent standards of living, Henry Ford made billions for himself and his family.

## CHARLIE PINNER: REWARDS IN ANOTHER CURRENCY

Not everyone is a Henry Ford and not everyone sees prosperity in strictly monetary terms. Charlie Pinner took his rewards in a different currency. In 1917, at the age of 21, he began his teaching career in a mountain school near Asheville, North Carolina. World War I called him to Europe in 1918. He returned from the war to complete his education, and continued to teach until 1922, when he became superintendent of schools in Wake Forest, North Carolina. Not many educators have the opportunity to serve as school superintendents at the age of 26.

But Charlie Pinner was interested in more than the nuts and bolts of running schools. To him, education was more than a business enterprise in which you wheedle revenue from school boards and budget funds for desks, books, erasers, toilet paper and teacher salaries (often in that order). Education was the exciting process of helping young people build their futures. Education was the process through which he could multiply his accomplishments many times over through the empowerment of his pupils.

So Charlie Pinner elected not to follow the dollar signs into the upper reaches of school administration. He chose to make a difference as the principal of a small high school in the small rural town of Tabor City, North Carolina. He came to Tabor City in 1937—three years before I was born—and devoted the rest of his 50-year career to imparting education to the children of my community.

Charlie Pinner never built a bridge, designed a building, authored a piece of legislation, founded a business, led a band or wrote a book. But the children he empowered through education went on to do all those things. One of them started her college career with a $100 donation from Mr. Pinner's pocket. She's the one who returned to Tabor City on a hot July day in 1976 to deliver the address dedicating the C. H. Pinner Library on the campus of the high school where he had been principal and she had been a student.

The high-school yearbook of 1957 was dedicated to Charlie Pinner. The dedication included Oliver Goldsmith's description of the village master in his poem, "The Deserted Village":

> A man severe he was and stern to view;
> I knew him well, and every truant knew . . .
> Yet he was kind, or, if severe in aught,
> The love he bore to learning was in fault. . . .

As I delivered the address at the library dedication, Charlie Pinner was there in the audience, and Goldsmith's words elsewhere in that poem seemed even more applicable:

> How happy he who crowns in shades like these,
> A youth of labor with an age of ease.

As these words are written, Charlie Pinner lives in retirement near his daughter in Rock Hill, South Carolina. He turned 95 on Sunday, April 14, 1991. No one has been more deserving of an age of ease.

# JOY THROUGH VOLUNTEERISM

Our involvement in causes greater than we are can extend far beyond the office doors, the factory gates or any other boundaries that define our work places.

When corporations look for individuals to lead their employees, they look for people who are willing to make a difference in their communities. People who show no interest in their neighbors are not likely to show a great deal of interest in their fellow workers. And if you're not interested in your fellow workers, how can you be interested in the company?

Every community abounds in volunteer organizations dedicated to doing good. Such organizations not only offer opportunities for service; they also offer opportunities for personal joy. Studies show that 85% of our joy as human beings comes from interacting with others. Only 15% comes from earned success or achievement.

# CARING AS A CAREER

It was through willingness to serve that the door opened for me to receive my doctorate. I was director of guidance at a junior high school in Columbia the year South Carolina desegregated its public schools. During the course of a tense summer, I became deeply involved in smoothing the transition from a segregated to a desegregated school system. In the process, I volunteered for community service in a number of areas, including counseling at the University of South Carolina.

My contacts with University of South Carolina people led to an invitation to enter the doctoral program. I worked as a graduate student in the role of an administrative assistant until I had finished my course work. Then I returned to the public schools while I worked on my dissertation. Later I took a job as instructor in the University of South Carolina College of Education. So by involving myself in a larger cause, I was able to attain my Ph.D. and open myself to wider opportunities.

I've been fortunate to have been involved in careers that call for interacting with others on a daily basis. Whether working one-on-one with problem children or speaking before large groups at banquets or professional meetings, I enjoy the interchange of ideas and feelings. The joy in my work would not be nearly so great if I did not see my careers in public speaking and education as opportunities to serve and not just opportunities to earn.

Were I in it strictly for the money, I would never enjoy the warm responses such as the one I received from James, a troubled child in Summerville, South Carolina. He was a first-grader, and something of a behavior problem. I was the school psychologist, so it was my job to test him to determine ways the school might help him. I kept in my office a jar full of little prizes—the type you get from Cracker Jack boxes. Children who stayed on task were rewarded with the opportunity to reach in and select a prize.

At the end of our session, I told James he could choose his prize from the jar. He examined its contents, then looked back at me.

"I want you," he said.

# WORKING WITH THE MENTALLY HANDICAPPED

I have found it particularly gratifying to work with the mentally handicapped, and it was my privilege in 1988 to address a Presidential Forum on the topic of integration of mentally retarded children into public schools.

Many people feel uncomfortable in the presence of people whose intellectual capacities aren't quite up to par. Many even think of them contemptuously, although that attitude is dying. My working with the mentally handicapped has led me to love and respect them.

I pay a team of mentally handicapped people to do my yard work. I pay them well, because they are conscientious and do a good job.

On occasion, I have experienced moments of pride over the accomplishments of mentally handicapped people with whom I have worked. I remember the time there was a Christmas parade outside my home. I rushed out to see it. The Boy Scouts had entered a float, and there on top of it was a high-school senior who had been in our program for the mentally handicapped. He was a member of an active troop in Conway, South Carolina, and he wore his uniform proudly.

I picked up the local newspaper recently to see a photograph of Trey, another mentally handicapped student, who was setting swimming records in a community partnership program with Coastal Carolina College near Myrtle Beach.

On one occasion, I was representing the Horry County school district at a meeting in Columbia when a familiar face appeared at the podium. The young man was not very articulate, but as he described his involvement with the Special Olympics, I remembered where I had known him. I had tested Frank in kindergarten when I was the school psychologist in Summerville.

When he was finished, I ran to him and he ran to me.

"Miss O'Tuel, look!" he exclaimed. "I got a high-school ring."

This is one of the great rewards of working with the mentally handicapped: watching them grow to the point that they can take their own places in the world. I've discovered that the handicapped can make it with the right blend of inspiration, determination and independence. In fact, studies have shown that among the educable mentally handicapped—those with IQ's in the 50 to 70 range—80% become contributing citizens, marry, and get good jobs. One study of 100 such students in Pennsylvania found that 86% obtained meaningful employment, 42% were making more than a first-year school teacher earned, and 50% had savings accounts.

## AN OPPORTUNITY TO VOLUNTEER

You don't need a degree in psychology or a career in education to experience the rewards of working with the mentally handicapped.

The Kiwanis Club in Conway is made up of business and professional people from all walks. Most of them have had little contact with the mentally handicapped. A few years ago, the club decided to fund a field trip for mentally handicapped students. They were to go by bus to the Riverbanks Zoo in Columbia.

Eight Kiwanians rode the bus with the students. They interacted with them and got to know them. It was a joyous experience for the Kiwanians and their guests. Now, whenever Kiwanians fund the field trips, they always stipulate: "We'll pay for the trip provided we can be there in the flesh. We want to see these students. We want to touch them. We want to care about them."

They're caught up in the joy of losing themselves in a cause bigger than themselves.

Are the mentally handicapped students the only ones who benefit from this?

Ask the Kiwanians. They'll tell you the benefits flow both ways.

# YOUR PLACE IN HUMANITY

Your efforts in behalf of others demonstrate a love for yourself as well. You cannot love yourself without having some concern for your place in the humanity. You secure your place in humanity by putting yourself at humanity's service. And because you're a part of humanity, you become not only the benefactor but a beneficiary as well.

I can think of few creatures more pathetic than those who go through life without once knowing the joy of helping others. The loftiest title, the heftiest bank account, the flashiest car and the most luxurious abode cannot compensate for the emptiness of a lifetime devoid of good deeds.

In the eloquent words of Sir Walter Scott:

*166*

## Make a Difference by 'Losing' Yourself

Despite those titles, power and pelf,
The wretch concentered all in self,
Living, shall forfeit fair renown,
And, doubly dying, shall go down
To the vile dust, from whence he sprung,
Unwept, unhonored, and unsung.

Those who lose themselves in causes larger than themselves are not truly lost. To find them, follow the footprints on the hearts of those who have benefited from their efforts.

# Chapter Nine

# *Goals That Glitter*

---

*If you settle for less than you can be, you will be unhappy for the rest of your life.*

*—ABRAHAM MASLOW*

When you set goals and determine to work toward them, things begin to happen. Goals focus your energy and your efforts toward an objective, the way a nozzle focuses the energy of a stream of water flowing through a hose. If you have goals, you don't wait for what the future will bring. You carve out your own future. Goals are your blueprints for living. Become aware of your possibilities, choose the goal you want to strive for, and go for it.

## EARNING A TYPEWRITER

As a young girl, I learned all the things I needed to know to become a rural housewife. I could cook a mess of turnip greens with the best of them, whip up a batch of biscuits, bake a passable cake and make banana pudding that would have you asking for seconds. I could sew a dress, mend a pair of socks and keep a clean house. I could hoe a row of beans, pick them, shell them, and cook them. I could stick sweet-potato runners into the ground, water them, watch them take root and grow and, come fall, dig them out of the ground. I could take them home, peel them, and turn them into a mouth-watering sweet-potato pie. I knew enough to make some farmer a good wife.

But that summer in Columbus County, I knew that I didn't want to become a farmer's wife. My goals lay beyond the kitchen, the barnyard and the dusty fields of growing crops. I wanted to put my fingers to work on something besides butterbeans.

So I set a goal. I would learn to type. I would become good at it. And that meant I needed a typewriter.

I found a good used Underwood for sale for $75. That was a lot of money for a farm family in the '50s. Dad and Mama had other priorities that seemed more important at the time. If their daughter married the right kind of man, she wouldn't need to learn to type.

But I set my heart on that typewriter. I made it my goal to acquire it. I worked all summer to earn the money, and I made it. I bought that typewriter and I learned to type. That old manual is still in my attic. It's obsolete in this era of computerized word-processors and laser printers, but it's a reminder to me that when you want something badly enough, when you set a goal to attain it, and when you work toward that goal, you're going to achieve it.

## THE FEMALE BUS DRIVER

Later, I decided to follow in the footsteps of my older brothers, Harold, Brooks and Wayland, and drive a school bus. I got a lot of ribbing about that. Back then, jokes about women drivers were considered hilarious and in good taste. That was before the high auto insurance premiums had brought home the fact that young girls as a group are safer drivers than young boys. I learned to drive and I learned to drive a bus. I got the job, and earned $33 a month— big money then for a high-school student. With it, I was able to buy material to make my clothes. No more dressing in feed-sack fashions. I was also able to buy my first watch and my first record-player—one with an automatic changer that played 45 rpm records.

# FINDING MONEY FOR COLLEGE

When my senior year was over, many of my friends were excited about the prospect of getting married and starting their adult lives. Not I. My goal, from the first day I walked into Miss McGougan's class, was to acquire an education. By the time I had graduated from high school, my teachers knew, and I knew, that I was college material. I wasn't sure how you went about getting into college, and I wasn't sure what it would cost, but I knew I wanted an education. My role model now was Beth Woody, my high-school English teacher. I wanted to be like her.

There was no college tradition in my family. My Dad had said that if the boys wanted to go to college, he'd try to borrow the money to help them. But why would a girl want to go spend all that money on an education?

When you set goals and determine to work toward them, things begin to happen. In those days before guidance counselors, I didn't know the process of selecting a college. But Mr. Pinner knew how to get me into that little college in Red Springs, North Carolina. And I found ways to add to that $100 "down payment," he made in my behalf.

The Pickett and Hatcher Educational Fund in Columbus, Georgia, was willing to make a student loan if I could bring in the co-signers.

Uncle Leon and my brother Harold were willing to sign the note, and I was on my way.

I also obtained several working scholarships in college. I went to an all-girl school, and meals were served family style. One of my working scholarships involved waiting tables in the dining room. I also obtained a library scholarship.

On week-ends, I'd go home to Tabor City, where I had a part-time job in H.G. (Doc) Dameron's drugstore. I began as a soda jerk, but soon began posting accounts and helping the pharmacist in other ways. Dr. Dameron offered to pay for my education if I would study pharmacy and come back to work with him in the business.

But I wasn't into science and math. I had made good grades in those subjects, but my heart wasn't in a career in pharmacy. My goal was to be a teacher like Beth Woody.

Even though I turned down the offer, Doc Dameron gave me employment throughout my college career.

# BLUEPRINTS FOR LIFE

I didn't know a great deal about formal goal-setting when I was making my way through high school, struggling through college and working toward my master's and my doctorate. But I was a natural goal-setter. When I set my heart on an objective, I was like a hound on a scent.

I know now that goals are the things that make things happen in your life. They focus your energy and your efforts toward an objective, the way a nozzle focuses the energy of a stream of water flowing through it. A water hose without a nozzle will wet a sponge if you hold the sponge under the feeble stream. But it won't accomplish much else. Put a nozzle on that hose, though, and it will knock the mud off the side of your car, knock down a wasp's nest under the eaves of your house and, if you have enough pressure behind it, stop a charging mob.

If you have goals, you don't wait for what the future will bring. You carve out your own future. Goals are your blueprints for living.

If you're a home builder, you don't go up to a construction site and say, "Hmmmm, I think I'll lay the foundation here, then put up some studs and see where that leads us." You decide ahead of time what type of house you want, you have a picture of it in your mind, you translate that picture into a detailed blueprint, and that's the house you build.

The same should be true with your life. You decide what you want to make of it, decide how you're going to accomplish it, and then you set to work making it happen.

When people complain, they always have a reference point. Somewhere out there is something better. Life will be better when they get a good boss, find the right mate, or get the kids out of the house and on their own. But things don't get better until you *make* them get better. The future is on its way, but if you want to control it, you have to act *now*.

## MAKE THEM *YOUR* GOALS

The goals you set should be *your* goals, and not those of somebody else. The goals you pursue should represent something you really want, not something you pursue out of a sense of duty or loyalty.

Had I adopted my parents' goals, I would probably still be shelling beans and scrubbing floors back in Columbus County, North Carolina. I would be miserable, and would be making everyone around me miserable. Those were not *my* goals.

Had I adopted the goals of Doc Dameron, my pharmacist employer, I would also have been unhappy. I am a "High I," and my joy comes from mixing with people, not mixing pharmaceutical drugs in a beaker.

When you follow someone else's goals, out of a sense of duty or obligation, you have to drag yourself toward the objective. This puts a drain on your energy, and you run out of heart and out of steam long before you achieve success.

When you pursue your own goals, though, you are propelled forward by your own zeal. You're like a rock out of a slingshot.

## AMBITIOUS BUT REALISTIC

Your goals should be ambitious but realistic. If you have a rubber arm and can't hit the side of a barn with a basketball, don't make it your goal to pitch for the Los Angeles Dodgers. If you're a grown woman with a 34-inch waist and a 32-inch bust, don't aspire to be Miss America. If you stand 5-feet-six, don't expect to make the NBA. But remember: There's a universe of challenging, worthwhile goals out there. Become aware of your possibilities, choose the goal you want to strive for, and go for it.

## WHEN JFK AIMED FOR THE MOON

The classic case of successful goal-setting was John F. Kennedy's challenge to Americans to put astronauts on the moon before 1970. It was an ambitious goal that would call for enormous effort and ingenuity. To get the astronauts to the moon and back safely would require equipment that had not been invented and technologies that had not been developed. At the time of Kennedy's inauguration, the United States was four months away from sending its first astronaut into space and 13 months away from putting the first one in orbit. The Soviet Union seemed to have a commanding lead in space technology.

Had Kennedy said, "We will put a man on the moon next year," his goal would have been unrealistic. Had he said, "Before 1970, we will be conducting manned exploration of other galaxies," he

*174*

would have been aiming for the impossible. But had he said, "Before 1970 we will develop a space craft capable of taking two astronauts into orbit at once," he would have been setting a goal that was too modest.

Kennedy's successors kept his commitment in mind, and American astronauts walked on the moon—in 1969.

# PUT YOUR GOALS IN WRITING

Successful people will tell you that the most effective goals are written goals. Write them down on a small sheet of paper, or on an index card. Make them brief, make them specific and make them positive. Don't write, "I'm going to lose 10 pounds as soon as spring comes and the weather is good enough to jog." Write: "By June 1, I will weigh 120 pounds" (or whatever the ideal weight is for your size and gender). Don't write: "I'm going to begin looking for a good job starting tomorrow." Write: "By January 1, I will have a job as an account executive with a major company at an annual salary of $35,000."

Once you've written your goals, put them at your bedside or in some other place where they will be constantly before you. Read them before you retire for the night and when you awake in the morning. That way, they will become embedded in your subconscious, and you will be alert for opportunities to turn your goals into reality.

# VISUALIZE YOUR GOALS ALREADY FULFILLED

Another way to sink them into your subconscious is to visualize their fulfillment. Through your mind's eye, see your goals already fulfilled. Let's say you're a woman, and your goal is to weigh 120 pounds by the time summer arrives. Visualize yourself walking down the beach in one of those Sports Illustrated swim suits. Observe the admiring looks of the men and the envious looks of the women. If you're aiming for that account executive's job, visualize yourself at your job, behind your desk in an impressive office. See yourself immaculately groomed, impeccably dressed, exuding poise and self-confidence. Visualize yourself entertaining clients in a posh restaurant, paying the tab with your Gold Card. Imagine yourself parking your sporty new car at your new address in that upscale neighborhood.

## IT PAYS TO ADVERTISE

Once you've determined what your goals will be, you may want to advertise them. By letting others know what you intend to do, you commit yourself to achieving the goals. You know that if you don't achieve them, you'll be wiping egg off your face. When John Kennedy made it the national goal to reach the moon before 1970, he didn't circulate it in a secret memo to his inner council. He made it known to the world. That gave the nation a strong incentive to reach the goal. When the Eagle had landed, there was no egg in sight.

When your friends know you're committed to a goal, they'll provide you with the extra encouragement and an occasional push toward the goal. Of course, 25% of your acquaintances will always be hoping you'll flop. But you can use them to advantage, too. Keeping them in mind will provide you with increased incentive to "show them."

## A DETOUR INTO TEACHING

I took a detour en route to my goal, and it could have been a permanent detour.

In those days, it was possible to teach school in North Carolina without a four-year college degree. After two years of college, I decided to obtain a temporary teaching certificate and take a teaching job. So in 1960, when I was still only 19, I signed my first teaching contract and, after turning 20, began teaching in a tiny high school in a rural area of North Carolina.

It wasn't an auspicious beginning. My heart sank when I first stepped into the room in which I would be doing my teaching. It was shabby and badly in need of paint. I asked the principal about getting it painted. He was on the brink of retirement, and not very enthusiastic about anything. He said the school couldn't afford a new paint job.

He didn't realize that he was not dealing with the genteel daughter of wealth and leisure. He was dealing with a farm girl who had slopped hogs, milked cows and painted barns.

I got on the telephone to the superintendent.

"If you'll provide the paint," I said, "I'll paint this classroom."

When I came back that next week, my classroom had been painted. And I didn't have to do the painting. The superintendent later came around who see who that spunky teacher was. I decided to show him the true meaning of spunk.

That first year, I had several students who were older than I. I taught all the English courses in grades 9 through 12. We had a total of 24 students in the senior class. In a school that small, you're expected to stick to the basics and pass up the frills.

But I was young and innocent, and also the protege of Beth Woody, the lady who had steered me onto the yearbook staff and into the Voice of Democracy contest. During my first year, the school produced its first yearbook and had its first Senior Day. I also decided that 24 seniors was quite a large enough group to stage a senior play.

The play was entitled, "A Ready Made Family." Somebody must have given the main character the traditional "Break a leg" encouragement. She did her best to oblige; she broke her foot the day before the opening. But she was a real trooper and went onstage anyway. And there in the front row was Beth Woody, my Tabor City role model. The play was awful, but Beth said it was great.

# MARRIAGE TO MAXCY, BACK ON TRACK

Maxcy O'Tuel had finished college the year I finished high school, and he was ready to settle down. I had postponed marriage to Maxcy while I pursued my college education, but after my first year of teaching, I finally said "yes" to his proposal. I finished the school year on Friday and we were married on Sunday. It was a simple but beautiful wedding. I made the bridesmaids' hats and had their dresses made. We moved to South Carolina and set up housekeeping.

Maxcy's parents were distressed that I hadn't finished requirements for my college degree. His mother was a schoolteacher, and his father, although not a college-educated man, had a deep respect for the value of education.

So, with their encouragement, I commuted the 60 miles to St. Andrews Presbyterian College in Laurinburg, North Carolina, three days a week and completed requirements for my bachelor's degree. Max and I moved to Darlington, South Carolina, the sleepy Tobacco-Belt town that was just awakening to the roar of stock cars on the track that was to make its name synonymous with big-time racing. I took a job at mid-year, teaching 8th grade math and science.

Don't tell me that eight-graders can't be intimidating. My third-period class consisted of 25 boys and five girls, and I can still remember some of the names. There were Donnie Outlaw ("Just call me 'Crook' "), Leonard Morse ("Call me 'Mullet' "—he worked after school at a fish market), Randy Gandy, Tommy Benton, Joe Carter, Toy Dutton, Jimmy Gainey and Carolyn Law. One day, as I was calling the roll, the class threw down the gauntlet: They had run off two or three teachers and they intended to run me off. I met the challenge with a mixture of firmness and nurturing, and I stayed. I left long enough to bear our first son, William, spent part of a year teaching in nearby Florence, then returned to Darlington. Two years later, Bryant was born.

# IF AT FIRST YOU DON'T SUCCEED. . . .

There's nothing magical about goal-setting. Once you set your goals, visualize them and make them known to your friends and associates, their achievement is not automatic. You have to work toward them, and you have to expect setbacks. But winners accept the setbacks as learning experiences. They take failure as a signal to try again, this time with a new tactic. They learn that success usually follows persistence. I found this to be true when I set out to expand my knowledge of math and science.

In 1963, I decided that if I was going to teach math and science in school, I should obtain more knowledge about the field. I received a federal grant to take some science and math courses at Memphis State University, so I seized the opportunity.

What I didn't realize—because the literature made no mention of it—was that I had to pass the Miller's Analogies Test before I could enter the graduate school at Memphis State. I was still a country girl who had never been anywhere. I had just flown from Columbia, South Carolina, to Memphis—my first trip west of the Appalachians. And I was pregnant with William. I did something I wasn't accustomed to doing: I flunked the test.

But my goal had been to take those courses, and I wasn't ready to admit defeat. I went to the dean and I explained the situation: I had met all the pre-requisites. Nowhere in the literature did it say I had to pass a test in order to take the advanced math and science courses for this summer program. The dean accepted me as a proba-tionary student. In engineering math and plant taxonomy—both gruel-ing courses—my grades were better than 99. I was the top student in both classes. There was no more talk about my being a probationary student.

# FROM MASTER'S TO DOCTORATE

My goals got higher. I won a scholarship to the University of Alabama, where I obtained a master's degree in guidance counseling. While we were in Tuscaloosa, Maxcy worked on requirements for his doctorate.

From Tuscaloosa, we went to Columbia, South Carolina, where we were to live for nine years. I taught 4th grade in an elementary school that first year, then became director of guidance in a new junior high school. That was the year South Carolina public schools were desegregated. We were in a very white suburb, and many or most white parents were irate over the busing plan, which called for inner-city blacks to be bused into their area. I made it my goal to make desegregation work. It wasn't an easy task, but I helped calm the strident voices in the white community and helped ease the transition for black teachers who were contending for the first time with white students and white parents.

I remember giving a baby shower in our home for Jeannette, one of the black teachers. She called me the next day.

"Is there a cross burning in your yard?" she asked.

There wasn't. Desegregation occurred relatively peacefully in the capital of the state that had led the South into secession. That year, I won the district Humanizing Award for my role in smoothing the transition.

It was during this stay in Columbia that Maxcy completed requirements for his doctorate and I obtained mine. Maxcy became principal of the largest middle school in the state, and things were quite stable for us. Then he received an offer as superintendent of a rural school district in Dorchester County, northwest of Charleston.

Maxcy accepted, and I obtained a position as school psychologist in Summerville, the largest town in the county, which was in a separate district. Maxcy's district was in danger of being impaired by the state. It was his job to bring the district up to standard. We were to remain there for more than a decade.

We decided to send the boys to school in Maxcy's district. We were living in that district, and Maxcy thought it would be hypocritical of him to send the boys to schools in another district. The boys were in full agreement. William had been in an accelerated program in Columbia, which the rural system couldn't match. As a result, William was far ahead of his contemporaries in Dorchester County and was advanced through the grades. He graduated at the age of 15.

Maxcy was just what the ailing school district needed. Before we left, his district had been cited as the most improved in the state and Maxcy was honored as the Outstanding Superintendent of the Year in South Carolina. I grew in my new position too. I became director of staff development in the Summerville school district, with responsibility for guidance services, public relations and other functions. My duties enabled me to get out into the community, working with the Chamber of Commerce to implement the Business Partnership between businesses and schools, and working with other organizations involved in building community spirit.

Those wonderful years in Dorchester County were brought to a close by Maxcy's health problems. In 1979, he became quite ill, and doctors diagnosed heart trouble. He underwent open-heart surgery and his aortic valve was given an artificial replacement. Max returned to work, but in the spring of 1984 the artificial valve had to be replaced. It was a close call. He spent three months in the hospital, including more than three weeks in intensive care. His doctors told him he should not return to his job. Max's career as a school superintendent was over.

To assure him of adequate care, we arranged for Maxcy to move into a beach house we owned in North Myrtle Beach, near his mother's home. I continued my position with the Summerville school system, commuting to North Myrtle Beach on week-ends to be with my husband. This continued for two years. Then I reached a decision: I would make it my goal to obtain a position in Horry County, South Carolina, to be near my husband.

I achieved that goal in the fall of 1986. We sold our beautiful country home near Harleyville in Dorchester County, and I accepted a position as assistant to the superintendent of Horry County Schools. Not only had I obtained a new job; it was a substantial promotion over my old one. I had gone from a school system of 10,000 students to one of 25,000 in one of the fastest-growing areas of the state. My responsibilities now covered 38 work sites involving 3,000 employees.

In Horry County, I would get my baptism by fire into school-board politics. I would be exposed to state-level educational issues and would find opportunities to develop my career as a professional speaker.

I did not enter this fascinating and rewarding career in a haphazard way. I made it my goal to address audiences, and I found myself speaking to people at all levels—from cafeteria workers to Ph.D.'s; from local audiences to presidential forums.

You too can achieve a rich and rewarding life by setting goals and working your way toward their achievement. Decide what *you* want to achieve. Write it down. Then make it glitter in your mind through the wonder of visualization. Always be alert for the next step to take you toward your goal. And work for it.

Don't be afraid of work. Work is not drudgery when it is directed toward something you really want. When I was a child, climbing a tree was not drudgery if it enabled me to reach the sweetest scuppernongs. When I was an adult, studying psychology was not drudgery if it helped me toward my advanced degree. To Michelangelo, chiseling marble was not drudgery if the goal in mind was a Pieta in Saint Peter's Basilica.

Your own life can become a masterpiece of achievement if you follow your goals to their fulfillment.

# Chapter Ten

# *Tap into Your Subconscious*

---

*The mind of man is capable of anything—because everything is in it, all the past as well as all the future.*
                                    —*JOSEPH CONRAD*

If you program your subconscious with negative thoughts, you will tend to act in harmony with those negative thoughts. Therefore, if you consciously perceive yourself as a failure, your subconscious will accept this information as valid, and you will act like a failure. If you believe you are a capable person, you will act like a capable person, and you will be able to accomplish the things you want to accomplish. If you believe that you are a good person, you will act in harmony with your perception. You will naturally do the things that you believe a "good" person should do.

# ALLY OR OBSTACLE

In Chapter Nine, we referred to ways of embedding your goals in your subconscious. Your subconscious mind can be a powerful ally in the achievement of your goals. Or it can be a powerful deterrent to success. It all depends upon how you program it.

What is your subconscious?

Henri Bergson referred to it as "the subsoil of the mind." It is the part of your mind that you're unaware of. Yet it exerts profound influence on the way you think and act. It's like the underground water table. You don't see the water, except where the ground level dips below the water table and lakes and streams appear. But it's there to nourish the crops that need moisture to survive, and it's there to provide water for domestic use if you want to drill a well down to the level of the aquifer.

# TWO LEVELS OF MIND

Students of human thinking say that the mind is organized into conscious and unconscious levels. The conscious mind is the one you think with. Through it, you are aware of your environment. The things you see, hear and feel enter your conscious mind. You draw conclusions and make judgments and decisions with our conscious mind.

The subconscious mind does all the things you can't be bothered with consciously. It functions whether you're asleep or awake. It keeps your heart beating, your lungs breathing and all your organs functioning. It controls your body temperature.

It also is the warehouse of your memories. You are not constantly aware of your office telephone number, the date of your wedding anniversary, the name of your fourth-grade teacher or where you left the book you borrowed from a friend. But when you need that information, you can quickly call it out of your subconscious memory.

If you compare your mind to a computer, your conscious mind is analogous to your monitor's display screen. Your subconscious mind is analogous to the disc on which your data is permanently stored.

# HABITS AND ATTITUDES

The subconscious mind also contains your habits and attitudes. Remember when you first learned to tie your shoes? You had to think through each step of the process. That was your conscious mind at work. But after you had done this repeatedly, the process became embedded in your subconscious. Now you can tie your shoes without thinking.

When you first get directions to a friend's house, you have to follow them step by step, turn by turn, carefully noting each landmark. After you've driven the route regularly, you make the turns unconsciously. The directions are in your subconscious.

Your subconscious receives its information from your conscious mind, and it never forgets. Suppose on your first trip to New Orleans the weather is foul, you catch a virus, your first meal of jambalaya disagrees with you and you become very ill. Your conscious mind tells your subconscious: "New Orleans is unpleasant. Jambalaya disagrees with me." Your subconscious logs this information. The next time you think of vacationing in New Orleans, your subconscious feeds the information to your conscious mind: "New Orleans is an unpleasant place. Better try Miami instead." The next time you see jambalaya on the menu, your subconscious tells you: "Jambalaya disagrees with me. Better try the stuffed flounder."

Your subconscious has been programmed with negative thoughts about New Orleans and jambalaya.

Perhaps your spouse or "significant other" prevails upon you to try New Orleans one more time. This time, the weather is pleasant, you have an exciting evening in the French Quarter, and in the exuberance of the occasion you try jambalaya one more time and love it. Now your conscious experiences are feeding new information to your subconscious. It revises its attitude toward New Orleans and jambalaya. The negative programming has been replaced with positive programming. From now on, you will enjoy New Orleans and jambalaya.

# NEGATIVE ATTITUDES

Negative attitudes can be fixed in your subconscious without your being consciously aware of them. Sometimes they stem from experiences of early childhood that you can no longer consciously recall. But your subconscious remembers, and these experiences color your attitudes and reactions. It organizes your attitudes and behavior around the facts as it perceives them.

Your subconscious cannot distinguish reality from perception. It knows only what your conscious mind tells it. It cannot check the validity of this information through direct observation. So if you want your subconscious to organize your attitudes and behavior in a positive way, you have to feed it positive information.

If you program your subconscious with negative thoughts, you will tend to act in harmony with those negative thoughts. Therefore, if you consciously perceive yourself as a failure, your subconscious will accept this information as valid, and you will act like a failure.

If you think you're going to have a headache, your subconscious will accept a headache as an inevitability, and you will develop a headache.

If you think a job is too big for you, your subconscious will believe you and you won't be able to get it done.

"Mind is the great lever of all things," said Daniel Webster. "Human thought is the process by which human ends are ultimately answered."

If you want your mind to exert positive leverage, you must

clear negative thoughts out of your subconscious and replace them with positive thoughts.

## THREE NEGATIVE CATEGORIES

There are three major categories of negative thoughts. They are:

** Worry. Worry is picturing, vividly and emotionally, life as you don't want it to happen. It's one of life's big wastes. We spend so much energy worrying about things that might go wrong that we fail to exert our efforts toward making things go right. Suppose Christopher Columbus had been a worrier. "Maybe the earth really is flat," he might have said. "We could sail off the edge in a few days and that would be the end of us. Or maybe it's round, but a lot bigger than we think. We could end up sailing on forever, with no prospect of replenishing our food and water." But Columbus didn't waste his energy worrying. He took a positive attitude: "The Indies lie somewhere to the west of us, and if I plot my course carefully and outfit my ships properly, we'll get there." I could have let worry defeat me when I was trying for those science and math courses at Memphis State. "What am I doing up here, pregnant and alone in a strange town? I've already flunked the test; why risk humiliation by begging the dean for a second chance?" But I have always programmed my subconscious with positive thoughts. They've pulled me through some tough and sad times.

** Guilt. Guilt is worry after the fact, and it's just as destructive as worry before the fact. We tend to blame ourselves for past decisions and actions as if fixing the blame would fix the problem. What's past is past. Dead and gone. If you've done something you now regret, stop punishing yourself. Tell yourself that you did the best you could, given the knowledge and abilities you possessed at the time. Bid your regrets good-bye, then move on toward positive goals.

### Lee at Gettysburgh

Have you ever done something you regretted? Sure you have. Have I? Sure I have. So has every other mortal who ever lived. Do you think Robert E. Lee didn't pause after Gettysburgh and say, "What if?" He had pinned his hopes for Southern victory on that engagement, yet had lost it in a muddle of miscalculations. But Lee went on to lend brilliant direction to the Confederate army until the North's superior numbers and resources made the struggle hopeless.

### Ike on D-Day

Dwight Eisenhower knew, when he ordered the invasion of Normandy, that he could be the goat of the European war by sunrise the next day. But he was willing to accept sole responsibility for the decision, knowing that he had done what he thought was best at the time.

### Truman and the Bombs

Probably no one on earth has been second-guessed more than Harry Truman, who ordered the nuclear bombing of Hiroshima and Nagasaki. Yet Truman said he never lost a night's sleep over it. He knew the decision meant the destruction of tens of thousands of innocent Japanese and intense suffering for others. Yet he believed he had done the right thing, given the information available to him at the time.

### Kennedy's Fiasco

John Kennedy didn't allow the fiasco at the Bay of Pigs to unsteady his hand when the Cuban missile crisis loomed.

Follow their examples. Don't dwell on the decisions of the past. If you made a bad call, acknowledge it, then forget it. Concentrate on making good decisions for the future.

** Grudges. One of the most positive, productive things any of us can do is to forgive the people who have offended us. If we don't forgive, our grudges smoulder away inside us. Like wet logs in a fireplace, they smoke up the place with their noxious fumes of hate without producing positive heat or light. My Aunt Bert was an example of what grudges can do for you. She carried a petty grudge against my father for years. Had she been willing to forgive, Dad's family might have shone the light of love into the last unhappy years of her life. But she couldn't forgive, and she died almost friendless. What a waste!

### A Two-Way Street

Forgiveness is a two-way street. Jesus taught us to pray, "Forgive us our debts as we forgive our debtors." When we forgive others, then we open ourselves to forgiveness. If we are unwilling to forgive, then we are unlikely to receive forgiveness. Few controversies are one-sided. If you hold a grudge against someone, chances are that person holds a grudge against you too. When you start the process of forgiving, the other person is likely to reciprocate. Remember, too, that if you are unable to forgive others, you probably are unlikely to forgive yourself.

# TECHNIQUES FOR POSITIVE PROGRAMMING

If your subconscious is willing to believe the negative things your conscious mind tells it, it is also willing to believe the positive things, and it will act in harmony with them. If you believe you are a capable person, you will act like a capable person, and you will be able to accomplish the things you want to accomplish. If you believe that you are a good person, you will act in harmony with your perception. You will naturally do the things that you believe a "good" person should do.

# POSITIVE SELF-TALK

One of the best ways to convince yourself that you're a capable, successful person is to tell yourself that it's true. You do this through a technique known as self-talk. Everyone engages in self-talk. It's the way people talk to themselves. You may not say things out loud, but thoughts are constantly running through your mind. Psychologists say you have about 50,000 thoughts per day—between 1,000 and 5,000 every hour. When you get up in the morning and say (or think), "Boy! This is going to be a lousy day; I can feel it in my bones," you're indulging in negative self-talk. If you say, "I can't wait to get to my desk and knock out that report," you're engaging in positive self-talk. If you say, "I know I'm good enough to handle the branch manager's job," you're using positive self-talk. If you say, "I'd like to get the promotion to branch manager, but I doubt if I'm ready for the responsibility," you're engaging in negative self-talk. If you make a mistake and say, "I knew it! I never do anything right," you're programming your subconscious for failure. If you say, "Okay, I did it wrong this time, but I won't make that mistake again," you're programming yourself for success.

If the three major categories of negative thought are worry, guilt and grudges, the three major categories of positive thought are confidence, love and forgiveness. Use these types of thought to program your subconscious through self-talk. Say nice things about yourself to yourself: "I like the color of my hair; it complements my complexion." "I don't know of anybody who can make a better sales presentation than I can." "I'm a caring and understanding person; I know the people on the new job are going to like me." "I'm going to wear my new dark pinstripe suit with the burgundy tie and pocket handkerchief, and when I go before the Planning Commission they're going to sit up and take notice." "So Phyllis beat me out for the sales manager's job. That's okay. I'm still a top-notch salesperson. I'm going to show Phyllis that I'm a good sport and help her set new records for the department. Who knows? If we work well together, we may be able to boost both our incomes."

You can program confidence into your subconscious by identifying, acknowledging and affirming your strengths. If you've ever attended a baseball game, you're familiar with the infield chatter. The infielders are constantly feeding words of encouragement to the pitcher. You're the pitcher. Be your own infield. Keep telling yourself how good you are and how confident you are that you're going to succeed.

Clarify your vision and your values. Where do you want to go? What is your purpose in life? What are the things that are really important to you? When you know these things, you can set goals and align your behavior with those goals. When your actions are in line with your purpose, you are a genuinely free person.

# AUTO SUGGESTIONS

Auto suggestion is a technique for telling your subconscious that you are what you want to be. The subconscious believes you and directs your attitudes and actions accordingly. When you say, "I am going to land a job as an account executive with a major firm and earn an annual income of $35,000," your subconscious believes you, and organizes your actions and attitudes *as if* you were sure of landing that job. It alerts you to the opportunities for obtaining that job. That newsstand you've been passing every day is no longer just a hole in the wall. It's a room full of possibilities. The Wall Street Journal on the rack is not just a mass of gray type. It's a directory of opportunity. The classifieds within it are no longer abstract notices. They are aimed at you. You buy it, you read it, you are alert for the type of job you want, and you apply. Meantime, every social and business contact becomes a part of your network of opportunity. Your subconscious prompts you to pick up on bits of conversation that might tip you off to opportunities.

Use auto suggestions to effect the changes you want to make. Write them down and repeat them over and over. If you prefer, write them down from seven to 21 times a day, or tape them and play the tape repeatedly. You can play the tapes while you're driving, while you're doing your household chores, and even while you sleep. You don't have to concentrate on listening. Just play them seven times and they will sink into your subconscious. Actors learn their lines this way, and students learn foreign languages this way.

Make your auto suggestions positive, and put them in the present tense. Some sample auto suggestions:

\*\* I have more energy.

\*\* I am more beautiful every day in every way.

\*\* I'm fantastic; I love myself.

\*\* I am independent.

\*\* I am powerful.

\*\* I am successful.

\*\* I enjoy my life and my relationships with others.

\*\* I'm well organized and always on time.

Remember that 80% of your success stems from attitude, while only 20% comes from technical skill.

But self-talk and auto suggestions won't *make* things happen. Only you can do that. So reinforce your positive programming with a plan of action. Then *do something* to make it happen.


# VISUALIZATIONS REINFORCE

Visualizations provide reinforcement for the written goals. Because your mind's eye "sees" you wearing the look of success, it directs your choice of clothing and guides your grooming. When you encounter the decision-maker who is able to offer you that $35,000-a-year job, you already look the part. You can also use visualizations to help you talk the part. Use your imagination to rehearse mentally what you will say and how you will act.

You may be amazed to learn that mental rehearsal is just about as good as actual rehearsing. A university in Australia conducted an interesting experiment with basketball players. It had 10 of them practice shooting baskets for an hour every day for 21 straight days. It had 10 others sit down, relax and *imagine* themselves shooting baskets and making each shot. The players who actually practiced improved their shooting average by 24%. Those who mentally rehearsed their shots improved by 23%.

You can use this technique for rehearsing a speech or sales presentation or for rehearsing a job interview.

Imagination is the workshop of the mind, and visualization is an excellent way to put it to work for you. Everything that has ever been created had to be imagined first. Automobiles, airplanes, radios, televisions, video games, computers and robots all had to be imagined before they could be created.

Program into your mind pictures of what you want to be, and put those pictures in the present tense. Keep those pictures constantly in mind. Don't expect the new "you" to appear immediately. It takes your mind 21 days to accept a change. So create the picture and work toward the reality.

## MENTAL TELEPATHY

Brains are like radio receivers and transmitters. They pick up and broadcast information. Duke University has done 100,000 tests on mental telepathy. It works! If someone doesn't like you, you feel it. You don't have to be told. On a job interview, you braincast your confidence or your lack of confidence. The interviewer can pick it up.

## CULTURAL PROGRAMMING

Negative programming often is a cultural thing. For years, women and minorities were held back through negative programming that told them certain achievements were beyond them. Generations of fine potential black journalists spent their lives in unrewarding vocations because major newspapers did not hire black reporters and journalists. Generations of fine black actors and actresses washed dishes and mopped floors for their livings because there were only so many "Steppin' Fetchit" and "Aunt Jemimah" roles. At the outset of his career, the album covers of country music singer Charlie Pride didn't carry his likeness because Pride was black and it was assumed that country-music fans would shun his music if they knew about his race.

By the same token, few women became lawyers, judges, CEOs, detectives, architects, engineers, airline pilots or truck drivers, because these were not "feminine" occupations.

The legacy has not been totally eliminated. If you are a woman, a black, a Hispanic or an Asian-American, your path to success may indeed be partially blocked by outmoded ideas.

That's all the more reason that you should *not* use the discrimination of the past as an excuse for failure or mediocrity. Ethnic and gender discrimination is a relic of the past, not a harbinger of the future. Choose the field in which you are qualified to succeed and in which you want to succeed and go into it as if you were naturally entitled to succeed in it. You are!

# GOVERNOR WILDER OF VIRGINIA

L. Douglas Wilder, the first black governor of Virginia, provided the example. Wilder did not campaign as a black man attempting to shed the shackles of the past. He campaigned as a mainstream Virginia Democrat who had earned the right to serve through years of experience in the Virginia Senate. He didn't do his campaigning in black neighborhoods. He went into the hills and hollows of Appalachia, where blacks seldom venture, and shook the calloused hands of coal miners. He didn't talk about civil rights and the bitterness of the desegregation era, when Virginia closed several public schools rather than admit blacks. He talked instead of law and order, the Right-to-Work law, taxes and abortion—the mainstream issues of the day.

Did Wilder's race hurt him? Undoubtedly. But it also helped him among some Virginians, who welcomed a chance to demonstrate the state's tolerance by voting for a black man with solid credentials.

# GENERAL COLIN POWELL ET AL

The national government is peopled with minorities whose abilities have been recognized by their peers. The overall military commander for Desert Storm was Gen. Colin Powell, chairman of the Joint Chiefs of Staff, who is black. Blacks have sat on the United States Supreme Court, have served in the United States Senate, have held high position in the United States House of Representatives, and have held Cabinet positions. Hispanics have served in the executive and legislative branches of federal government, and on the federal bench. California's San Hayakawa and Hawaii's Daniel Inouye and Spark Matsunaga have shown that Asian Americans can reach positions of respect in the national Congress.

# WOMEN LEADERS

Women too are gaining positions of influence in government, serving as state governors, U.S. senators and representatives, Cabinet members, diplomats, and agency heads. A woman now sits on the U.S. Supreme Court, and a woman has run for vice president on a major-party ticket.

In journalism, William Raspberry and Clarence Page are among the nation's leading syndicated columnists, Ed Bradley is a familiar face on CBS' 60 Minutes, and Bernard Shaw has gained respect as the news anchor for Cable News Network. Ellen Goodman, Anna Quindlan, Flora Lewis and other fine columnists have shown that women can succeed in journalism.

## STAGE, SCREEN AND ARENA

Women, blacks, Hispanics, and Asian-Americans are no longer novelties on the local television news sets. In the movies, Sidney Poitier blazed a trail for black actors playing the role of heroes, and the trail is by now well-trodden. Bill Cosby showed that blacks could be funny without being stereotypical. When Jackie Robinson broke the color barrier in professional baseball, the minorities swarmed in. Being black isn't the least bit of hindrance in becoming a basketball star, and even deep-South college coaches vie for the services of the Herschel Walkers and Refrigerator Perrys of the gridiron.

## DON'T SAY 'WHAT'S THE USE?'

So if you're female, black or a member of some other racial or ethnic minority, don't say "What's the use?" The field in which you want to succeed has probably long since been opened to people of your race, gender or ethnic category. If it hasn't, give your subconscious a firm and positive statement: "I'm going to be the next Jackie Robinson or Sidney Poitier or Douglas Wilder; the next Sandra Day O'Conner or Geraldine Ferraro or Connie Chung."

Say it, visualize it and believe it. You can accomplish what you want to accomplish if you believe in yourself. After all, look who became the first female student bus driver at Tabor City High School in North Carolina.

## DEVELOPING INTUITION

Have you ever had an idea come to you "out of the blue"? Some of the greatest discoveries of all time have come about in this way. The ideas seem to come from nowhere. Actually, they come from a part of the brain that some scholars call the "superconscious." Others consider it to be a part of the subconscious. Regardless of how you look at it, we all have the ability to produce ideas through inspiration or intuition. The ability to fashion ideas without going through the logical reasoning process is a remarkable faculty of the mind.

Our brain functions through two hemispheres—the left brain and the right brain. We generally use the left brain when we are doing mathematics, reading a research report, drawing a blueprint or performing some other task that calls for logical reasoning. With your left brain, you can reason from cause to effect, and vice versa. If you see ripples forming concentric circles in a lake, you can reason that an object has fallen into the water. You see the effect, so you can figure out the cause. If you see rain falling outside, you know that you'd better bring your clothes in off the line. You see the cause, so you can figure out the inevitable effect on your clothes.

The right brain functions in a different way. It takes new information, runs it quickly over its subconscious storehouse of old information, makes a comparison, and reaches a conclusion. You are not conscious of a reasoning process. You have a "hunch," and so you act upon it. Or suddenly, with no apparent mental effort, the solution to your problem appears.

## LOGIC AND CREATIVITY

The left brain is generally associated with logic, while the right brain is associated with creativity. You learn a language through your left brain, but you write a poem through your right brain. A left-brain quarterback will stay in the pocket; a right-brain quarterback will scramble. A left-brain general will go by the book; a right-brain general will improvise.

All of us have the capacity to use both hemispheres of our brains. But most of us prefer one side over the other.

In a sense, right-brain and left-brain people can be compared to the tortoise and the hare. Right-brain people do quick scans of their subconscious memories and attitudes and go with their feelings. They are like the hare, darting here and there, skipping among the various solutions until they find one that accords with their sense of what is correct. They rely on their intuitions. They learn through flashes of insight.

Left-brain people believe that "slow but sure" wins the race. They'll reason: "Since this is true, it follows that thus and so is true." They acquire knowledge through this form of deductive reasoning. Some tasks require the use of the left brain. You're not likely to find the square root of 5,280 by using your right-brain intuition, unless you've already worked it out in your left brain and stored it in your memory. You're not likely to compose a great symphony through left-brain reasoning. You have to compose through your creative right brain.

# THE TREASURE HUNT

If a left-brain person is looking for buried treasure, he will make a grid of the area to be searched, develop criteria for determining the most likely site of the burial, rank the squares on the grid in the order of likelihood, and painstakingly and systematically excavate the area in order of rank.

If a right-brain person is looking for buried treasurer, she will select a spot where her intuition tells her the treasure may be. She is not digging blindly, although she might not be able to tell you why she's digging there. But her mind has unconsciously scanned the area and selected the site where her subconscious tells her the treasure is most likely to be buried. Perhaps she knows the person who buried the treasure and therefore has stored away information on the way that person thinks and responds. Or perhaps she has had some experience at hiding things in the ground, and that experience guides her in choosing the spot to dig. She will not have the patience to follow the left-brain person's logical procedure.

Who will be the first to find the treasure?

It all depends upon the volume and reliability of the information stored in the right-brain person's subconscious.

## INTUITION NEEDS INFORMATION

When right-brain and left-brain people of equal intelligence with an equal fund of information take a test, the right-brain people are likely to finish first, although their scores will be no higher than those of the left-brain people.

The right-brain person's hunches are reliable only to the extent that they are based upon an adequate fund of information. If the right-brain person hasn't used the left brain to gather and store information in the subconscious, then the right brain's conclusions may be faulty.

Left-brain people tend to be interested in the world as it is. They seek to understand why things are as they are.

Right-brain people tend to be interested in possibilities. They wonder why things can't be the way they want them to be.

Right-brain people are good at generating ideas. Left-brain people are better at executing them. Einstein's intuition led him to the theories of relativity, although it took left-brain logic to prove their validity. It's a rare individual whose capacities to imagine and to execute are both highly developed.

If you are a left-brain person, you can get in touch with the intuitive side of your mind through the process of meditation. To do this, find a quiet time of day and a quiet place where you can be comfortable and relaxed. Shut out all distractions. Turn off the television set, unplug the telephone and get comfortable.

Then set your mind free to wander. If you have a problem on your mind or a decision you need to make, don't try to reason it through. Just let your mind roam easily and positively over the situation. Often, when your mind is rested and you're at peace with yourself and with the world, this kind of meditation can produce marvelous insights.

Intuition often comes when you least expect it. Many successful people keep notepads handy at all times so that when an idea strikes "out of the blue" they can write it down before they "lose" it. Many writers use this technique to capture their best lines.

When Thomas Edison got stuck on a problem that seemed unsolvable, he would take a short nap. When he awoke, the solution would often come to him. Many discoveries come as hunches after intense periods of study and research followed by a nap or a period of relaxation. It's always good to sleep on a problem at least one night.

If you're a right-brain person, remember that your intuition is only as good as your information. Information enters the subconscious mind through the conscious mind. So put both sides of your brain to work. Stock your left brain with a healthy fund of information. Let your right brain dream dreams. Let your left brain provide the blueprint for turning your dreams into reality. Then apply the blood, sweat, toil and tears to the execution of that blueprint.

# Chapter Eleven

# *The Testimony Is in Your Footprints*

*If this is my day of harvest, in what fields have I sowed
the seed, and in what unremembered seasons?*
*—KAHLIL GIBRAN*

You can't leave footprints while you're standing still.
To make tracks, you have to move. If you expect to
influence people, you have to model the behavior you'd
like to see in them. So clear away the lethargy, despair
and doubt within you and act as if you were motivated.
Radiate enthusiasm. When you're walking across
people's hearts, you have to be careful. Footprints can
be gentle or rough. They can soothe or they can irritate.
The way you motivate people determines whether the
footprints you leave will be welcome or unwelcome.

## PLANTINGS AND HARVESTS

Life is a continuum of plantings and harvests. We give of ourselves, either generously or sparingly, and we receive in corresponding proportions. As we stride the furrows of life, the footprints we leave tell whether we are making a casual pass through the field or are taking the time to make a difference. Are the impressions deep from sharing the burdens of our fellow workers, or shallow from steps gingerly taken lest our shoes get stained with the dust of life? Is the path straight, because we walked through without looking to left or right? Or are there signs that we paused to pull a weed here and there, straighten a bent stalk, apply the balm of nurture to a languishing life form? Do our footprints show that we cared, or that we just fared?

To leave lasting footprints, we have to show love, and love is not a passive, detached thing. It requires action and involvement. On his death bed, Richard Rodgers, the great composer, found these words to express the idea to Mary Martin, the star of his Broadway hit, "South Pacific":

> A bell is no bell till you ring it.
> A song is no song until you sing it.
> Love in your heart
> Wasn't put there to stay,
> It's nothing at all
> Unless you give it away.

## FOOTPRINTS IN SEASONS PAST

The memorable tracks that we make are not impressions in the literal soil, but footprints on the hearts of those we touch. And sometimes we leave them in seasons unremembered. I recall the time I placed a phone call to an elementary school with which I had worked many years before.

"May I speak to the principal?" I asked.

"Is this Mrs. O'Tuel," came the voice.

I was astounded. It had been seven years since I had set foot in that school. I was sure no one on there would remember me.

"Would you tell me who you are?" I asked.

"I'm the maid," she said. It was July, and at that time of the year few people are around the school to answer the telephone.

What enabled her to remember my voice after so many years?

I had left footprints on her heart just by caring about her and showing an interest in her. For one year, my office had been located in that school while the district offices were being renovated. Every morning she would come into my office. Every morning I'd say hello. Then I'd say something like, "You know, you really make a difference at this school. I like the way you clean this area."

When I realized why the memory of my voice had remained so long with this woman, I told myself: "I'm going to be good to people as long as I live, because you never know when you're leaving footprints on their hearts."

I remember receiving a letter from Johnny Odom, whom I had taught 22 years earlier. He told me he had become a construction worker and had made something of himself because of my influence as his sixth-grade teacher.

On another occasion, when I had returned to make a speech in Darlington, I encountered Brenda Pipkin, whom I had taught in 1964. She told me that she had become a teacher because I had been her role model.

It has been tremendously uplifting to learn that what Beth Woody and Anne McGougan did for me, I have been able to do for others.


# TITLE OR TESTIMONY?

I am grateful to Tony Campollo for preserving the words of a black minister in Pennsylvania, who distilled in a few sentences the wisdom that rings from Genesis to Revelation:

Brothers and sisters, you are going to die. They will put you in a hole and throw dirt in your face and go back to the church and eat potato salad. When you were born you were the only one to cry. Everybody else was happy, rejoicing, laughing, and celebrating. When you die, will you be the only one who is happy and those about you crying? The important question is, "When you die will you have a title or a testimony?" . . . Do you want those at your funeral talking about your title or do you want them giving a testimony about what you have meant to others during your life?

Pharaoh had the title, but Moses had the testimony. Jezebel had the title and did all she could to destroy Elijah, but in the end Elijah had the testimony. Nebuchadnezzar had the title; Daniel had the testimony. Pilate had the title, but my Jesus had the testimony. When they hang up your sneakers, throw dirt in your face and go back in the church to eat that potato salad, what will it be? Title or testimony?"

## YOU HAVE TO MAKE CONTACT

So how does one obtain the testimony?

You cannot influence people for good or bad unless you make contact. An episode from the story of Bambi stays vividly in my mind. The young Bambi was standing on the edge of a meadow when he saw a battle-scarred old stag with majestic antlers striding along the opposite edge.

The young deer said to himself, "How I'd love to talk to that deer. Just think of all the experience and knowledge he has. He knows where the food is. He knows what to avoid. He knows all about life."

But Bambi never tried to make contact.

"He doesn't have time to fool with me. I'm just a kid," he said.

The stag, meanwhile, was looking toward Bambi and thinking, "What I'd give to be a young buck again. Wouldn't it be wonderful to talk with him just to get a perspective on life through his eyes. Wouldn't it be nice to experience his freshness and find out what's going on with his peers." But then he thought, "No. That young fellow has better things to do than take up his time with an old stag."

I think of that episode when I see someone I'd really like to interact with. I'm not afraid to say, "I'm Muriel. I have a question for you. Would you mind giving me a few minutes?" If the person is busy, I'll say, "Well, when can I see you?" Or "Would you give me your phone number? Would you give me a card?"

You can't leave footprints while you're standing still. To make tracks, you have to move. If you expect to influence people, you have to model the behavior you'd like to see in them. So clear away the lethargy, despair and doubt within you and act as if you were motivated. Radiate enthusiasm.

When you're walking across people's hearts, you have to be careful. Footprints can be gentle or rough. They can soothe or they can irritate.

## THREE WAYS TO MOTIVATE

The way you motivate people determines whether the footprints you leave will be welcome or unwelcome. There are three ways to motivate:

** By force. Adolf Hitler, Benito Mussolini and Josef Stalin were masters of the use of force. All three lie unwept, unhonored and unsung. When you motivate by force, you have to establish your own superiority and the inferiority of those you're dealing with. That leaves rough and painful footprints on the heart.

** By manipulation. You con people into doing the things you want them to do. That means using trickery and deception. This method runs afoul of the old Chinese wisdom: "Do me once, shame on you; do me twice, shame on me." Manipulation is effective only in the short run, if it works at all. The person who has been manipulated feels humiliated and cheated. Footprints left through manipulation are irritating on the heart.

** By positive persuasion. This is the process of sharing thoughts, opinions and knowledge. Knowledge changes perspectives, and perspective influences behavior. Positive persuasion can be accomplished only in an atmosphere of reason and logic. If people respect you, they will be more likely to follow you. You will leave positive and soothing footprints.

Positive persuasion is the more long-lasting and effective of the three. It begins with a positive attitude and with an expectation of success. It works by making people feel important. Persuasive people are those who give others status; who give recognition for the things others do right; who are constantly encouraging others, and who communicate freely and honestly.

## BUILDING ESTEEM IN OTHERS

Remember that about 90% of what people do is prompted by the desire to feel important. There are a number of ways you can make others feel important. Here are some of them:

** Be accepting. You must accept others totally and without judgment. You must accept those who are different from you. It's easy to accept people who are like you. It's harder to accept those who march to a different drummer. But remember: The world was designed to accommodate a variety of personalities and talents. If we'd waited for Beethoven to invent the automobile, we'd still be riding horses. If we'd waited for Henry Ford to write a symphony, the best we'd get would be the sound of a car horn. We need artists and artisans, dreamers and doers, generals and diplomats. Accept people for who and what they are. Advertise your acceptance with a smile.

** Show approval. Be generous with your praise. When someone does something that pleases you, praise that specific act. Praise is most effective when given intermittently and immediately after the desirable act.

** Show appreciation. Say please and thank you, and treat others as if they were guests in your home. Compliment people on what they're wearing, on the appearance of their offices, and on other things you admire about them. But be sure your compliments are true and sincere.

** Never criticize. Negative criticism is destructive and it's something the receiver never forgets.

** Never argue. When you argue with someone else, you're saying, "You're wrong," and nobody wants to be told that.

** Listen. When you listen to what others have to say, you'll find out what they value and what they like. Listening builds character in the listener.

Building others' self-esteem is the key to happy interactions with others. And interacting with others is a key to your own happiness. Studies show that 85% of human joy comes from getting along with others.

# ENTHUSIASM FUELS SELF-ESTEEM

To get along with others, you have to get along with yourself. If you don't like yourself, others certainly won't like you. And you won't like others either.

To feel good about yourself, you need enthusiasm. Have you ever noticed how infectious enthusiasm is? Athletic teams play better when they're performing before a home crowd. Why? Because the enthusiasm of the crowd imparts enthusiasm to the team.

Winston Churchill's enthusiasm, communicated eloquently to the British via BBC, helped rally his beleaguered nation against the Nazi onslaught.

On the day after Dunkirk, when British forces had been evicted from the European continent, when Hitler was the master of all Europe from the Oder to the Atlantic, when America was still hoping to avoid war with Germany, when Russia was still digesting the portion of Poland it had seized under the pact between Hitler and Stalin, and when Britain alone, its army beaten, its cities vulnerable, stood in defiance of the Axis, the prime minister told his people:

> We shall not flag or fail. We shall go on to the end. We shall fight in France, we shall fight on the seas and oceans, we shall fight with growing confidence and growing strength in the air, we shall defend our island, whatever the cost may be, we shall fight on the beaches, we shall fight on the landing grounds, we shall fight in the fields and in the streets, we shall fight in the hills; we shall never surrender!

Does that sound like a man whose forces have just taken a licking? That kind of enthusiasm primed the British nation for its finest hour and kept it alive and kicking until America joined its might with the land that had given it birth.

Enthusiasm does more than conquer tyrannies. It is a maker of friends. It tells people, "I've got what it takes." People want to follow and emulate those who have what it takes.

Enthusiasm, wielded skillfully by a salesperson, turns "no" into "yes"; in the hands of a corporate executive, it turns waste into productivity; loss into profit.

## SEVEN QUALITIES OF LEADERSHIP

You exude enthusiasm when you think positively about yourself and act in a confident manner. You can provide a solid basis for that confidence by developing the seven qualities of leadership:

** Integrity. This is the quality that attracts the confidence of others. It embodies the qualities of dependability, uprightness, honesty and loyalty. The word comes from the Latin word "integer," which means "whole" "untouched" or "entire." To have integrity is to remain unshattered, unwavering, sound and incorruptible.

** Perseverance. This is the quality that persists in the face of difficulties; that never acknowledges defeat; that keeps an eye on the goal and tries again and again to attain it.

** Faith. Strong leaders are firmly convinced that something better lies ahead. They believe in the ultimate triumph of right. They believe that problems arise to test us, not to thwart us. "Faith," declares the writer of He

*211*

brews, "gives substance to our hopes and makes us certain of realities we do not see."

** Ability to plan. It does no good to have good ideas and good intentions if you don't have the ability to plan. Ability to plan involves a knowledge of the facts, judgment as to their relative importance, mastery of the job, skill in organizing to accomplish a purpose, and efficiency in coordinating the work of others without showing off or showing them up.

** Vision. This quality calls for a breadth of view—the ability to grasp the big picture. The leader with vision is able to play not just for today but also for tomorrow and for the next generation.

** Initiative. This is the ability to move ahead without waiting for a shove. Good leaders are self-starters who see what needs to be done and set about getting it done. They are trail-blazers whose footsteps mark the paths for others.

** Courage. True leaders are risk-takers who are willing to take chances on losing because they know they have the spunk to try again. Courageous leaders instill courage in those around them.

## FOOTPRINTS IN THE FAMILY

Your life is full of opportunities to leave footprints on hearts. The path starts in your own family. You can leave indelible footprints on the hearts of your children through the values you inculcate in them.

Among those values is that of responsibility. The mother of Dwight Eisenhower sent her six sons into the battle of life with these instructions:

You must do your duty, and after that you can do anything you want, provided it's decent.

We can leave footprints on our children's hearts by exposing them to awareness of the manifold opportunities that confront them. Too often, we abdicate our parental duties to the television set, to video games or to other forms of diversion. We let gadgets become their surrogate parents.

A long time ago, before the generation gap became a yawning chasm, parents and children spent time together out of necessity. I remember the way it was on our farm. Without VCRs, television sets and one automobile per capita, families had to stick together.

# FIRESIDES, ICE CREAM AND BOILED PEANUTS

On winter evenings, two or three generations of kinfolk would gather around the fire, and the ancient art of storytelling was practiced. There, we learned our family folklore and absorbed family values. There were woven the ties of common heritage that bound one generation to the other.

On summer days, we'd hold similar sessions around the ice cream churn, communicating across generational lines while the churn turned ever more slowly and the creamy-smooth milk absorbed the fresh fruit in its cool embrace.

On other days, we'd do our family socializing around a black wash pot filled with water and fresh-picked peanuts. The Northern palate has not yet discovered the glorious taste of the boiled peanut, but we knew about it in southeastern North Carolina. We'd pull the peanut vines from the soft soil, shake the sand from the roots, and pluck the succulent legumes off. Into the pot they would go, along with a generous dousing of salt. We'd light a fire under the pot, and wait until the boiling heat had softened the shells and cooked the nut to the consistency of a boiled pinto bean. And as we awaited the magic moment, we communed with each other.

# TAKE TIME TO COMMUNICATE

It's a little more difficult these days to achieve that kind of communication. It's hard to transmit folklore and family values while gathered around a microwave. And when we try to do our communicating during prime time, our voices are drowned out by the noise of the tube. That's why it's important for parents to set aside definite time periods each week to get to know their children, to talk to them and—above all—to listen to them. Do not use these times to watch television together.

When God gave Moses the Ten Commandments, he told him:

> These commandments which I give you this day are to be kept in your heart; you shall repeat them to your sons, and speak of them indoors and out of doors, when you lie down and when you rise. Bind them as a sign on the hand and wear them as a phylactery on the forehead; write them upon the door-posts of your houses and on your gates.

# CONFLICTING VALUES

In another time, the values embodied in the Ten Commandments were universally accepted, though not universally practiced, in our culture. When parents spoke these words at home, they could expect them to be repeated in the schools, in the churches, at the corner drugstore, at the grocery store, at the barber shop, at the beauty parlor, and even over the air waves.

Today, the message our children receive at home is just one of a bewildering tangle of messages. The mass media long ago bade farewell to the Ten Commandments and became tools of persuasion for every saint and charlatan who learned how to use them and manipulate them. Unless we communicate to our children in strong, clear, persuasive and loving language, the chances are great that they will be seduced by other, less wholesome messages.

As we give them our messages, let us remember that as time passes, our own experiences may seem less and less relevant to what our children are experiencing. There was a time when parents could communicate to their children the sum total of their own experiences, and these experiences would be relevant to the children's generation. But the pace of change has become so great that when one generation attempts to interpret its experiences to another, it's hard to find a common language. Language differences can be overcome if each party takes the trouble to listen carefully to the other. Parents need to listen to their children.

# ENDURING PRINCIPLES

Though the stream of change alters values the way floodwaters alter the landscape, there are core values that are impervious to time. Love for others and a willingness to serve humanity are never outdated. There are other enduring truths as well.

Our children will be much more attuned to technology than we have been, but we can teach them those lasting verities. One of them is that technology is not civilization. Technological gadgets are the artifacts of civilization. The electronic keyboards reproduce sounds, but the music does not come from the gadgets. It comes from the minds of composers. The most remarkable instrument of all is still the human brain, with its ability to communicate across space and time. We still see the Mona Lisa through the eyes of Da Vinci, and we still relive the Battle of Troy through the songs of Homer. The Theories of Relativity on which nuclear technology is based were worked out by a human brain connected to nothing more complicated than a pencil and pad.

We can teach our children that though the 20th century has multiplied knowledge, it did not invent it. This generation launched the rocket, but the generations that preceded it slowly, painstakingly, built up the launching pad. Neanderthal people were probably no less intelligent than 20th century people. They didn't build automobiles because they didn't have the tools. Therefore, they invented tools so that we could build automobiles.

It is good for our children to learn to use a computer, learn to operate a VCR and learn to match wits and reflexes with video games. But it's also good for them to know about Homer and Virgil, Alexander and Cincinnatus, Socrates and Maimonides, Beethoven and Verdi, Shakespeare and Faulkner, Roosevelt and Churchill. They need this awareness of their cultural roots in order to appreciate fully the rich web of opportunity that confronts them on the brink of the 21st century.

They need to have inculcated in them the bedrock principles of morality embodied in the Sermon on the Mount. These principles do not erode with time and do not evaporate in the heat of change. In an age in which much that glitters is plastic, they represent pure gold. Make sure your children know how to mine them.

# ENCOURAGEMENT IS VITAL

Our children need something else from us: encouragement. Growing up in the shadow of the arms race, in the throes of cultural change, in the mine field of the drug culture, they need assurance that there's hope out there; that the American dream still lives; that happiness is still a commodity in abundant supply.

They need to know they're loved, totally and unconditionally. They need to know that their parents believe in them; that they are valued as human beings in their own right and not as reflections of Mom or Dad or some older sibling.

It will help if you remember what it was like to be a child yourself. The further you distance yourself from this memory, the harder it will be for you to understand your children. You know what turns young people on, because you remember what turned you on. Let them know that you know who they are. Let them know that you know what they like. Let them know that you know they're human. Let them know that you're human too.

# YOUR CHILDREN ARE NOT CLONES

In our age, even more than in previous ages, it can be disastrous to pressure children into following in parental footsteps. They will be living in a totally different world. We can't chart their paths for them; the best we can hope to do is to equip them to chart their own. Our children will be much happier pursuing their own goals than they would be pursuing ours. In the words of Kahlil Gibran:

> You may give them your love but not your thoughts,
> For they have their own thoughts.
> You may house their bodies but not their souls,
> For their souls dwell in the house of tomorrow, which
> you cannot visit, not even in your dreams.
> You may strive to be like them, but seek not to make
> them like you.
> For life goes not backward nor tarries with yesterday.[3]

We can send them into the future with positive images of themselves. We can applaud their accomplishments, praise their strong points, and gently and lovingly show them the way to overcome or compensate for the areas in which they are not strong.

---

[3] Kahlil Gibran, *The Prophet,* (New York: Alfred A. Knopf, 1972) p. 17.

# WHO IS SPECIAL TO YOU?

How often we forget that our children are special people. When our son Bryant was a sophomore at The Citadel, he used to come home each Sunday, bringing three or four of his classmates with him. So Sunday after Sunday I would cook a big dinner—roast beef, potatoes, chicken, the works. After several weeks of this, I said, "Bryant, it's nice having your friends over, but I need a break. Why don't you just come home next Sunday and relax without all those other guys here. Let's just share some time together."

"Mama," he said, "I like to bring my friends because when they're here you cook things I like. You have roast beef or baked chicken, you fix dessert, we eat in the dining room, you put a tablecloth on the table. And you look better too. You dress better when they're around. I like the way you treat me when the guys are here. You smile more. You even smell better."

Bryant was making a valid point: I was doing special things because of his friends, when I should have been doing them because of him.

# HEALTHY DISCIPLINE

Our children need our discipline—not the harsh lash of punishment, but the firm but loving direction that guides their growth in positive ways.

Loving discipline supplies a structure to life. It gives children the security of boundaries. Children who grow up with that kind of love and discipline have a natural sense of well-being that others have to work to achieve. They are self-confident. They have poise and self-esteem.

Some students of human behavior theorize that a loving structure at home provides that same kind of contentment a child experiences when it cuddles in a parent's arms. When a child is thus cuddled, its body secretes endorphins, those substances that have a mild, soothing effect on the brain. A child who grows up in an endorphin-producing environment develops a healthy ability to produce endorphins throughout life. A child deprived of an endorphin-producing environment may grow up in need of outside stimulation to achieve the same feeling of well-being.

Whatever the validity of that theory, the effectiveness of love in promoting good mental and physical health is well documented. One of the most effective and pleasant therapies known to humanity is the simple hug. It's effective for adults as well as for children.

Hugging is miracle medicine. It can relieve many physical and emotional problems we face. It can help you live longer, protect you against illness, cure depression and stress, strengthen family relationships, and even help you sleep without pills. Research indicates that when a person is touched, the amount of hemoglobin in the blood increases significantly, and this tones up the whole body.

Hugging is a tonic. It breathes fresh life into a tired body and makes you feel younger and more vibrant. If you're having problems in a relationship, try applying daily hugs. They can reduce friction and strengthen the relationship.

Astonishingly, many people don't know how to hug, or at least they feel inhibited when it comes to hugging. They substitute various types of non-hugs. Some examples of non-hugs are:

** The A-frame. In this non-hug, the heads touch, but not much else. The feet of one partner are about 3 feet from those of the other, and the torsos sort of bend toward each other, forming the outline of a pup tent.

** The half-chest. I call this the "One Boob Is Better Than No Boob" hug. The partners sort of assume a side-by-side position, touching at only one corner of the chest. It's as if they fear a full-chested confrontation might be considered licentious. Baloney!

**     Chest-to-chest burp. This one is a big hit with women. They go chest to chest, all right, but there's no genuine feeling. One partner pats the other's back in a perfunctory manner, the way she pats a baby to burp it.

**     Wallet rub. This is worse than the half-chest. You just stand side by side and touch hips.

If you really want your hug to do you and your partner some good, look the other person directly in the eye, use both arms, fold the partner in your embrace and put all your love and affection into the hug. Don't be afraid to touch. That's what starts the endorphins to flowing and the hemoglobin to pumping.

So if you want to give your children a healthy start in life, hug them often, and hug them heartily. Use the technique on family and friends as well. You'll leave warm, soothing footprints on their hearts.


# FOOTPRINTS IN THE COMMUNITY

We can leave footprints on our communities as well. In my home town, Charlie Pinner's footprints have been memorialized through the library that bears his name. His footprints were laid down quietly but indelibly.

Community service is an important way of marking our passage. It has given me some of the most rewarding experiences of my life, and has enabled me to leave footprints wherever my career has taken me.

I have already related how community service in Columbia provided me with an entree to the doctoral program at the University of South Carolina.

In Dorchester County, it helped me establish contacts with the business world through the Business-Education Partnership, which I spearheaded, and through work with the Chamber of Commerce and other community-spirit organizations.

When I left Dorchester for Horry County, I continued these interests. I've continued to promote the Business-Education partnership in Horry County schools, and I'm active in many other areas, including:

** The Advisory Board of Citizens Against Spouse Abuse.

** The Board of Directors and Allocations Board of the Horry County United Way, which I also serve as Education Division chairman.

** The Board of Directors of the Conway Chamber of Commerce.

** The Board of Directors of Family Support Services and chairman of its CAMEO Awards Program, a recognition program for working mothers.

** The Equity and Access Commission for Horry Georgetown Technical Education College.

** The Horry County Human Relations Council.

** The Horry County March of Dimes, which I have served as division chairman.

** The Board of Visitors of Coastal Carolina College in Conway and of Presbyterian College in Clinton, South Carolina.

** The Horry County Department of Mental Retardation, Case Study Advisory Board.

Governor Carroll Campbell also appointed me to the South Carolina Commission on Business/Education Partnership for Excellence

*221*

in Education and I was appointed to the Education Year 2000 Task Force for the State Department of Education by Dr. Barbara Nielsen, state superintendent of education.

These are not just honorary positions; they're working positions to which I devote many voluntary hours.

# FOOTPRINTS IN HARLEYVILLE

You may think it's pointless to volunteer for community service unless you possess some area of expertise. That's not the case at all. Remember that in the kingdom of the blind, the one-eyed person is supreme. We discovered that when we moved from Columbia to Harleyville, South Carolina, when Maxcy became superintendent of the school system there.

Columbia is a metropolitan area of 430,000 people, with all the human resources one would expect of a city that size which also happens to be the state capital and home of the state's largest university.

Harleyville is a town of 400, which means that when the O'Tuels moved there, they immediately increased its population by 1%.

Harleyville is not a religiously diverse community. Basically, you have two choices: You can go to the Baptist Church or you can go to the Methodist Church. Bryant, our younger son, made friends with some Methodist kids, so he started attending the Methodist Church. The rest of us went to the Baptist Church, since that was the denomination we had been affiliated with in Columbia and it was also the denomination that Max's mother believed to offer the surest route to salvation. Bryant's "defection" certainly was no cause for agony on our part. The chasm between Baptists and Methodists is by no means as great as that between Shi'ites and Sunnis in Moslem lands. In fact, when the Baptists held a revival, everybody in town went to the Baptist Church. When the Methodists had their revival, everybody became Methodists for a week. It was a friendly sort of sectarianism, and once you'd got past the baptism (sprinkling for Methodists, dunking for Baptists), the theological differences were not great.

## BRUSHING UP ON THE 'BLOOD SONGS'

The choir in our Columbia church was about half as large as the entire congregation in Harleyville. The Harleyville choir consisted of six to eight people, none of whom could read music.

I had taken piano lessons as a child. Ergo, when the choir directorship became open, I was quickly anointed. I practiced my piano a bit, brushing up on the "blood songs" ("Washed in the Blood," "Power in the Blood"). Soon I was playing for revivals—something I would never have found the courage to do in Columbia.

## AN INTRODUCTION TO THE DULCIMER

My musical career took a new departure one summer when I was looking for something to do to get away for a break. I was scanning a bulletin from Appalachian State College in Boone, North Carolina, where Maxcy had received his master's degree. There I saw an item about a dulcimer workshop.

A dulcimer, for the uninitiated, is a stringed musical instrument that is part of the folk heritage of Appalachia. Having been reared on the coastal plain, far from the Blue Ridge Mountains, I knew nothing about it. So I signed up for the course.

I returned to Harleyville refreshed, bursting with music, and carrying a dulcimer. Harleyville is located deep in the heart of the South Carolina Low Country, so the folks there had never heard of a dulcimer either. Soon, I was called upon to give a mini-concert at a revival. The concert must have been well-received, for shortly afterwards I was invited to give a recital before the Book Club in Harleyville. The Book Club was an organization you belonged to if you wanted to keep abreast of culture.

## 'WHISKEY BEFORE BREAKFAST'

The Book Club engagement enabled me to expand my repertoire beyond the "Blood Song" genre of the revival meetings, and I felt pretty good about the performance until I read the account of it in the local newspaper. The item read: "Mrs. O'Tuel played a selection of songs on the dulcimer. Among them were 'Amazing Grace' and 'Whiskey Before Breakfast.' "

They were a forgiving crowd at both churches in Harleyville, and I didn't lose my choir directorship over this detour into the profane. In fact, I continued to present the program for the Women's Missionary Union the first Monday of each month. There were quite a few older women in this church group, and it was a challenge to draw them into participation. They preferred that I inform them, entertain them or inspire them while they remained passive listeners. They especially enjoyed the gourmet liqueur coffee I served when the meeting was at my house.

## A VARIETY OF FOOTPRINTS

Perhaps the people of Dorchester County, when they think of Muriel O'Tuel, will think of "Amazing Grace" played on a dulcimer. Perhaps they will think of "Whiskey Before Breakfast." Or perhaps they will think of the wisdom and humor I imparted through those women's programs, my efforts in behalf of community development, or my efforts as a school psychologist to help children and parents understand themselves and each other.

There were footprints left when I headed the United Way campaign in Dorchester County schools. There were footprints left through the organization of a community resource group, which enlisted the cooperation of the Commission for Mental Health, the County Commission on Alcohol and Drug Abuse, the Department of Social Services, the Chamber of Commerce and the YMCA. There were footprints left through service with the Exchange Club Center for Sex Abuse Prevention, the PTA regional board, the executive board for exceptional children, the school-intervention program, and others.

I have left footprints through my work in promoting racial harmony. A black friend, The Rev. Robert V. Leeper, pastor of the Brownsville Church of God in Summerville, gave this testimony about me in a letter to the superintendent of Horry County schools:

> She relates extremely well with various races and ethnic groups as well as all ages and persons of either masculine or feminine gender.

And I left footprints as a female pioneer in a masculine preserve, as attested to in an editorial entitled "Thanks, Muriel" in the Summerville newspaper:

> She was the first woman hired for a district-level post, among the few who wasn't from the ranks of coaching, and certainly one of the few here who did not drive a pickup truck.

## YOU CAN START SMALL

My experience in Dorchester County can provide a model for those who feel lost in large organizations, where only the most accomplished experts among the membership are privileged to make a contribution. Seek out small organizations, where each member counts. You may find that your own talents are valuable and welcome. And you may find in these organizations an opportunity to hone your skills for later application in larger arenas.

Your interests and talents may lie in directions quite different from mine. But whatever your inclination, your community needs you. Go serve it. You will make permanent footprints on the hearts of those you serve.

# FOOTPRINTS IN THE WORKPLACE

Finally, you can leave your footprints on the places where you work. Regardless of where you fit on the corporate chart, you can influence your organization and your fellow employees in negative or positive ways.

There are several sources of power in the work place. One is the formal power that a person holds by virtue of position on the corporate chart. The people over whom you have formal power are expected to follow your instructions because you have the authority of the organization behind you.

Another source of power is the respect others have for you. If people like you, admire you and see you as a role model, they will follow your lead.

A third source of power is knowledge and expertise. When people believe that you're the person who knows how things are done, they'll come to you for information and guidance.

Through the exercise of formal power, we may accomplish specific tasks. But it is through the power of respect and through knowledge and expertise that we leave footprints on the heart. To exert these twin powers, we have to share what we know, and we even have to share our authority.

## THE POWER OF RESPECT

How do you gain that coveted power that comes from the respect of your peers? You have to act like a leader. That means, first of all, that you have to approach your job with a positive attitude. When you do this, your confidence and optimism radiate out to your fellow workers. When they absorb it, they become more effective, and this effectiveness shows up eventually on the bottom line.

You will not be able to exhibit that positive attitude unless the job you're doing challenges and stimulates you. If your objective when you go to work in the morning is to get through the work day so that you can begin living *after* work, you're not going to succeed at your job.

Remember what we learned in Chapter Four: Each of us has traits of temperament and personality that affect the type of work we will enjoy and will do well. Identify your own behavioral style and seek out a career that will enable you to function freely within your behavioral style. You will thus be working with the wind to your back.

## SIX STRATEGIES FOR OPTIMISM

In his book, *The Power of Optimism*,[4] Alan Loy McGinnis, director of the Valley Counseling Center in Glendale, California, gives these six strategies for cultivating optimism:

** Attach yourself to hopeful people. Make sure the optimists outnumber the pessimists in your circle of acquaintances. As an optimist, you'll want to show loving concern for those who think the world is down on them

---

[4] Alan Loy McGinnis, *The Power of Optimism*, (New York: Harper & Row, 1990).

and try to boost them toward optimism. But you'll need optimistic companions to keep recharging your batteries.

** Change your intellectual patterns. British statesman Benjamen Disraeli said that "all other things being equal, the person who succeeds will be the person with the best information." Make a tour of the non-fiction shelves at your public library. Pick out some fascinating books on philosophy, history, science. Turn off the tube, open a book and savor the knowledge it offers. Will it help you directly in your career? Maybe not, but it can do wonders for your powers of concentration and it will make you feel better about yourself. By the way, how much has "Three's Company" helped you in your career?

** Feed your spiritual side with care. McGinnis says he sees few atheists among the go-getters. If you start to feel pessimistic about the future, try renewing your spiritual roots or cultivating some new ones. Read and think about your faith. Above all, pray. When George Washington Carver, the great scientist and inventor, was stumped on a project, he would break off his work and pray. A solution would emerge.

** Talk to a young child. Children are natural optimists, and it's impossible to remain depressed in a room full of healthy, lively children. One of the saddest developments of our time is the emergence of retirement communities where families with children are not permitted to live. I remember the charge of optimism I received when a youngster said to me, "I wish you were young like me so we could grow up together."

** Make use of the ancient idea of the Sabbath. Even God found it useful to rest after six days of work. Find opportunities to take a break to renew family, personal and spiritual ties and give your body a chance to relax.

** Get to know somebody new. Teachers should not just talk to teachers, lawyers should not just talk to lawyers and husbands should not just talk to wives. Find ways of connecting with someone in a different walk of life, a different age bracket, a different cultural background. You will gain refreshing new insights that will boost your optimism.

# DARE TO TAKE RISKS

The optimism you exhibit will enable you to take risks. No one respects a coward and nobody follows the fainthearted. But the risk-taker must be willing to accept responsibility for mistakes. When you make a mistake and accept the responsibility people won't condemn you for the mistake; they'll commend you for taking the responsibility. Then your positive attitude will help you to fail forward—to learn from your mistake and build upon your knowledge.

To lead, you must set goals. Nobody wants to follow people who don't know where they're going. Goals mark the trail you intend to follow to success.

To lead, you must take the initiative. How can people follow you when you aren't going anywhere?

# LEAD BY EMPOWERING OTHERS

One of the ironies of life is that you gain power by giving it away. On a football team, the quarterback will lose consistently unless he frequently passes the ball or hands it off to another player. By passing or handing off, he empowers his teammates, and they multiply his power. Be willing to hand the ball to others. Cheer them when they run for the goal. Praise them for their gains. Encourage them to try again when they're thrown for losses.

If you yield formal power, you will find that the people under your supervision will respond positively to opportunities to contribute to the team. Workers don't like to spend their days performing routine, repetitive tasks. They want to be able to think and have their thoughts appreciated. Companies who encourage this kind of thinking on the part of line workers benefit in the form of practical and ingenious ideas as well as more loyal, more committed work forces.

## JOINING THE CORPORATE TEAM

You can empower others even when you don't wield formal authority. How? By sharing with them your own knowledge and expertise.

In the work place of the future, everyone will be expected to be on the corporate team. From the worker monitoring the assembly-line robots to the CEO maintaining communications with a global network of branches and suppliers, everyone will be expected to work in alignment with corporate goals.

So as a member of the corporate team, you will not be concerned just with your work station or your department. You will be looking for ways to improve team performance at all levels. You will see your job as part of the total picture, and not as an isolated function. It will no longer be "I'll stick to my job and you stick to yours." It will be "Let's work together to see that my work and yours make an effective contribution to corporate goals."

In the old days, supervision valued the assembly-line worker who could install a door panel in perfect alignment. But if you had 100 workers installing door panels and only one was doing a quality job, it meant that 99% of your door panels were poorly installed. In the new work place, management will value the assembly-line worker who can teach and motivate the 99 other workers to do their jobs with quality.

So your success in the future may well depend upon your ability to get the best out of others as well as out of yourself. This means sharing unselfishly the knowledge and skills you acquire, empowering others to bring their performance levels up to—or even ahead of—yours.

When you do that, you will discover a wonderful thing: Other people have abilities too, and they'll be willing to share them with you. By working as a *team* instead of as lone rangers, you will be able to put quality into your company's products or services and value into your own contributions.

# RESPONSIBILITIES OF SUPERVISION

If your role is in supervision, your responsibility toward others becomes even greater. You have an opportunity to leave footprints as a role model for those you supervise. Many middle-management people create problems for their companies and their employees by setting negative examples. One survey of management people in the United States, Great Britain, Australia and New Zealand showed that 85% worked 45 hours a week or more, 83% worked through lunch at least once a week, 65% worked at least one week-end a month, and 47% spent three hours or more a week on business work at home.

Burning the candle at both ends might have made a good impression on Ebenezer Scrooge. But enlightened management knows that the person so consumed by the job probably doesn't know how to manage time effectively, and doesn't know how to delegate. Furthermore, such people are probably spending inadequate time with children and spouses and may be building up family problems that eventually will have an impact on their job performances. Managers such as this are good at building up inventory: the inventory of stress.

Moreover, they are passing along a message to their employees: to get ahead in this organization, you've got to work through lunch, work overtime on the job, and take your work home with you. Now, instead of just one stressed-out manager, you have a whole department of stressed-out employees, each building up troubles at home that will eat away at job performance.

## THE JOY OF MENTORING

Perhaps the best way to leave footprints on the heart in the work place is through mentoring. Some companies have formalized mentoring programs through which newer employees are assigned to work closely with more experienced people.

But you don't need a formal program to become a mentor to someone else. Look for someone with less experience than you who might benefit from the things you know. Take that person under your wing. Become a friend and confidant. Take every opportunity you can to point the way to success. The reward will be great for the protege. But it will be even greater for the mentor. There's nothing quite so exhilarating as seeing someone you've coached and taught go on to success. I'm sure that on the evening my first class of seniors presented the school's first senior play, my high-school English teacher and role model, Beth Woody, got even more pleasure out of the event than I did.

## THE LANGUAGE OF VALIDATION

One of the great joys in life is to hear words of validation coming from someone you've helped. I want to spend a little time on validation, because it's an important concept.

Sometimes when people do things for us, we fail to express our gratitude. It isn't because we don't feel thankful. We just take it for granted that they *know*. Then time passes, people get older, and the words of gratitude don't get said. Soon we realize that our benefactors have passed out of our lives without ever having heard the words that express our feelings toward them.

Take time to express words of validation to those who have left footprints on our hearts. You can do it within your family on special occasions such as birthdays and holidays. Christmas is a wonderful time to do it. You can the give gift of validation, and it won't cost a dime.

Sidney Simon teaches us that the language of validation involves four wonderful words. The first is "appreciate." The second is "admire." The third is "respect." The fourth is "love."

To give the gift of validation, set your benefactor in a chair opposite you, look the person in the eye, and say things like this: "I appreciate all you've done for me this year." "I admire you for the way you always care and show your care." "I respect you for being a great role model." "And I love you."

I'm grateful that I have had the opportunity to stand before both Anne Brooks McGougan and Charlie Pinner and express words of validation. My career as a speaker set up both opportunities. I saw Miss McGougan when I returned to Tabor City to speak at the dedication of the C. H. Pinner Library in 1976. The story of how she introduced me to Humpty Dumpty has become the signature story in the speeches I give.

# THE LOVE FEAST WITH CHARLIE PINNER

I got my opportunity with Charlie Pinner in 1990, when I went to Rock Hill, South Carolina, to address a group of state leaders during a guidance conference at Winthrop College. I knew that my former principal had retired to Rock Hill and was living there near his daughter.

It was between 9 and 9:30 in the evening before I was free of my speaking duties, and I wondered whether it might be a little late to call Mr. Pinner. After all, he was in his 90s by now. I called him anyway.

"Mr. Pinner, this is Muriel Ward O'Tuel, and I'm over at Winthrop College. I'd like to come and see you."

I could detect the excitement in his voice.

"I'm in my pajamas, but I'll put on my house coat and I'll wait for you."

It took me a while to find the house, but after I got there, we both enjoyed a love feast. I hugged him, then gave him a long, loving look. He seemed so short. I had remembered him as being taller and bigger. I realized that his leadership and his large role in my life had given him stature in my eyes as a school girl.

As we talked, I learned for the first time that when he introduced me to the president of Flora Macdonald College it was not the act of one professional talking to another. The principal and the college president had known each other for many years, starting with the days when both worked at a mission together while Mr. Pinner was a superintendent in the Wake Forest area. Mr. Pinner was cashing in a friendship in my behalf.

I also learned of his service in World War I, his studying at the University of Paris, his graduation from Mars Hill College in 1917, and his appointment as superintendent of the Wake Forest schools in 1922. He had made quite a name for himself at a young age, and had gone on to dedicate 38 years to making proteges of the young people of Tabor City and vicinity.

On that occasion, I made sure that the words "appreciate," "admire," "respect" and, above all, "love," were part of my conversation.

I know what those words must have meant to Charles H. Pinner, because I know how sweet they sound to me when I hear them from family, friends and proteges.

# CLOSING WORDS OF VALIDATION

So with your indulgence, I will close this chapter with words of validation toward people who have been my family, my mentors, and my valued friends throughout my life and career:

To my mother and father, Rosa and Zeddie Ward, who gave me the gift of life, who instilled in me the work ethic, who provided me with a strong moral foundation, and who imparted to me the good health that comes from a wholesome upbringing. . . .

To my brother Harold, who nurtured me like a third parent, who helped me over so many of the obstacles of childhood. . . .

To Anne Brooks McGougan, who opened my eyes to the joys of education and the wide, wonderful world to which it leads. . . .

To Beth Woody, who encouraged me to make the highest and best use of my talents and who provided for me a healthy and wholesome role model. . . .

To C. H. Pinner, who served as a leader and guide during my high school years, who provided the key that opened to me the gates of college, and who put substance behind his love with a generous contribution to my education. . . .

To Mildred and Bryant O'Tuel, the wonderful in-laws who encouraged me to complete my education and to reach out for goals beyond a bachelor's degree. . . .

To Maxcy O'Tuel, who gave me a wonderful marriage, two handsome and loving sons, and the support and nurturing I needed to pursue triple careers as mother, educator and public speaker. . . .

To Bryant O'Tuel, my younger son who grew up strong and brave and handsome and proved the source of so much parental joy. . . .

And to all those too numerous to name whose footprints rest soothingly on my heart, whose love and encouragement through the years have sped me down the road to success and achievement. . . .

Let me at this opportunity say, "I appreciate you, I admire you, I respect you, I love you."

And to my older son, William: Let me pour out my language of validation in an epilogue that I know will reach you and gratify you and multiply the happiness that I am confident is yours.

# *Epilogue*

*Those who do not know how to weep with their whole heart don't know how to laugh either.*

*—GOLDA MEIR*

My Christmas letters are a chronicle of pride. They tell of the growing, the reaching, the maturing of a family of achievers. I will begin, William my son, with excerpts from my letters, beginning with the Christmas when you were a second-grader in Columbia:

**December 1970.** Our 7-year-old William is a creative second-grader who seems extremely pleased with his black teacher. This is the final year of kindergarten for Bryant, and he readily admits that he will be glad to be in "real school" like the rest of us. William still manages to outwit Bryant, but Bryant's ever-loving disposition permits such. We take them camping at every opportunity and they thrive on outdoor living.

**December 1975.** Scouting has been a big thing with our 12-year-old William this year. In his first year with Boy Scouts he has come from Tenderfoot to the rank of Star Scout. Several camp-outs and a 50-mile hike adventure were highlights for him. He is now in beginner band with a new trumpet. William and Bryant's

latest project is a chicken house and yard. They have completed
the structure according to plans they drew and are now working on
the surrounding fence. Their Christmas list includes 15 laying hens
for Bryant and a pig for William.

**December 1976.** This bicentennial year has brought the first
teen-ager into our household. William maintains a busy pace at school,
with agriculture and chemistry as special subjects. He has completed
the requirements for the Eagle Scout Award, which he is to receive
in January.

**December 1977.** Each year of Low-Country living brings us
closer to the native status. William and Bryant have the dialect
down pat, but Max doesn't own a pick-up truck with a gun rack
yet. William's muscles kept the lawn mower humming this summer
and at last our yard has that "cared-for" look. He received the
Eagle Scout Award early in '77 and attended his first National Scout
Jamboree in Pennsylvania in July. A special highlight was his being
selected to attend the National Order of the Arrow conference with
six other Scouts from South Carolina. (He said the highlight was
seeing "Miss Teen-Age America). His most challenging school subjects include drafting and biology.

**December 1978.** William's year has been full of highlights despite
a bout with hepatitis last spring. He attended the Governor's School
for Scholars at the College of Charleston this summer, which he
found quite stimulating. He remains active in Scouting and was
elected vice-chief for administration for the Muscogee Lodge in South
Carolina.

**December 1979.** Our most significant happening was William's
going away to college in August. He was the recipient of a full
academic scholarship to The Citadel which (according to his dad)
was an offer he couldn't refuse. Adjusting to The Citadel's fourth-
class system is some process (especially for a 15-year-old) and Wil-

liam declares that the life of a freshman "knob" is no joy ride. William worked on the Camp Barstow Scout staff all summer and was one of the chief Indian dancers for the Order of the Arrow ceremony, which was televised. With William at The Citadel in Charleston, we spend as many week-ends there as possible. (William has no overnights). We have fallen in love with the charm of this beautiful old city—its cobblestone streets, theaters, churches, harbor, etc. St. Matthews Lutheran Church is our favorite place for Sunday worship.

**December 12, 1980.** William is much more relaxed as a sophomore at The Citadel this year. He holds the second-highest rank in his company, with a promotion effective second semester. Scouting remains a vital part of his life. At a conclave of lodges from North and South Carolina, he won first place in the individual Indian dance competition with Superior Premium rating for the authentic Indian costume he hand-made. He worked on the staff at Camp Barstow for six weeks this summer and was awarded the Vigil Honor at a special ceremony. He was also elected chief of the Muscogee Lodge, Order of the Arrow, which entails many administrative duties. We are delighted that he plans to take a ski trip during the holidays to get away from it all.

**December 1981.** William is a junior majoring in biology and has the rank of platoon sergeant. Although his first semester has been a heavy, he continues to make time for scouting on a state/ national level. He was re-elected as chief of Muscogee Lodge, Order of the Arrow, and this summer he worked as a commissioner at Camp Barstow near Columbia, where his main responsibility was serving as a liaison between the scoutmasters and the camp director. At the National Jamboree in Virginia he worked as an assistant scoutmaster. I'm convinced that scouting is in his blood forever. Both William and Bryant look forward to a week of snow skiing in the mountains of North Carolina the first week in January. (P.E. college credit was their selling point to us.)

**December 1982.** William's senior year at The Citadel is a full one, with his being selected for the Summerall Guards, Honor Court and Academic Officer. He attended Army ROTC Camp for six weeks this summer at Fort Bragg, North Carolina, which he said is enough Army for him. Scouting is still on his agenda with his being elected section chief (South Carolina, North Carolina and Georgia) in the Order of the Arrow. In July, he and Bryant went on a 10-day backpacking scouting expedition to Philmont, New Mexico. By the time this letter reaches you, the four of us will be on a five-day cruise to the Bahamas—the best Christmas gift idea we could think of. It sure beats cooking!

**Christmas 1983.** William graduated from The Citadel in May and is now enrolled in Medical School, University of South Carolina. His first-year curriculum is extremely demanding and he studies hours daily. Last spring William was elected national vice-chief of the Order of the Arrow, which means attending seminars, planning sessions, etc. throughout the United States for two years, representing more than 145,000 Order of the Arrow Scouts and their leaders. He spent the summer working at the National Boy Scouts of America headquarters in Dallas, except for one month's interning with Senator Strom Thurmond in Washington. This fall he was named by BSA as one of four 1984 national youth representatives. In this capacity he will make the annual BSA report to President Reagan in February on behalf of 4.5 million Boy Scouts.

**December 1984.** William continues to adjust to the demands of the University of South Carolina School of Medicine, which translates into STUDY, STUDY, STUDY. He took time off last February to meet with President Reagan and Congress to present the Boy Scouts of America's annual report. Most of this summer was spent at North Myrtle Beach getting a taste of the world of work and finding out his meager salary barely paid the rent.

*240*

**December 1985.** William is still hitting the books (sometimes the books win) as a medical student at the USC School of Medicine. He and two classmates rented a house in the Shandon section of Columbia, so they have arrived. Last summer he worked in the lab at Richland Memorial Hospital. He thoroughly enjoyed this experience and decided that drawing blood isn't bad once you get used to it. The tough part was having to punch in at 5 A.M.

**December 1986.** William has shown much interest in medical research and was delighted with the opportunity to assist the graduate dean (USC School of Medicine) with a cardiac research project with emphasis on arteriosclerosis. We pray for breakthroughs that can benefit Maxcy as he copes with this dreaded disease. Maxcy says William must have more experience and data before he'll participate in his project.

It is our prayer that this season will be a time of real joy and gladness for you and yours and a prelude to a Happy New Year.

Do you remember the February of 1970 when you and Bryant and I were on the way to school and a woman driver disregarded a stop sign and hit the right front side of our car? I went through the windshield and Bryant hit the dash. In the ambulance on the way to the hospital, I was feeling distraught and depressed when Bryant looked up at me and said, "Mommie, aren't you glad we're not dead?"

How grateful I was that we were safe and that a little care and attention at the hospital would make us all whole again.

After December 21, 1986, I have wondered whether we would ever be whole again. It was your father who got the call. I was packing at the house in Dorchester County and he had just returned to Myrtle Beach from Fort Rucker, where Bryant had graduated from flight school. When he got the call, he came to find me.

You were dead, William. Gone suddenly, inexplicably from our lives. We could not guess why. Your bag was packed for a trip to Memphis. You had entertained some friends over the week-end, and had consumed some alcohol. That morning, you were feeling very poorly—from a hangover, everyone guessed. They did not know you were allergic to alcohol. They could not guess that, in the loneliness of your suffering, you would reach into your white medical jacket for the drug you used to put the lab rabbits to sleep. They did not know (did you?) the lethal effects of that injection into a bloodstream already contending with the alcohol that had poisoned it the night before.

The authorities ruled it accidental suicide. We are left with the pain that always accompanies a tragic and unnecessary death.

But we are also left with pride in you and the footprints you left on countless hearts during your young and active life.

And I am left with these reflections on death and grief:

** God has entrusted to us a very great sorrow. Its depth is so great that it will not heal of itself. Only through God's help can the wound be healed.

** The loss of a child is the ultimate loss. It is so unnatural for parents to bury their children.

** The loss of a loved one is a lesson in vulnerability; it teaches us that we have no guarantee against losing the people and things most precious to us.

** Grieving people lose their sense of omnipotence and innocence. They never fully regain it. Their ability to cope with life is impaired.

** We do not easily become desensitized to old experiences. Emotional pain from the past has a tendency to return again and again. I ache for all the great things that you were and for all the great things that you were on your way to becoming. But most of all, I ache for the bright, adventurous, loving and lovable child I knew for 23 wonderful years.

** It is not one's duration of life that counts, but one's donation to life.

** We progress slowly, but we move in and out of the stages of grief.

** Scars remain. Our view of the world is colored by past experiences. As the weight of sorrow descended, I found myself identifying with the thoughts expressed in this prayer:

I am empty, Father. I am bitter, even toward You. I grieve, not only for the one I have lost, but for the loving part of myself that seems to have died as well. You, who have at other times brought the dead back to life, revive my dead ability to love, to be close, to care about this world and those I know. I believe, I insist, that You can heal this mortal wound.

** To survive, to love, and to laugh again, we must keep our faith strong. I draw strength from some words of faith I once read that were scrawled on the wall of a cellar in Cologne, Germany, by an American who was hiding there with some comrades after escaping from a German prisoner-of-war camp. The inscription read:

"I believe in the sun, even when it is not shining;
"I believe in love, even when feeling it not;
"I believe in God, even when He is silent."[5]

Only those who have felt a loss of this magnitude can appreciate the aptness of the expression, "heavy heart." In the agony of grief,

---

[5] Walter B. Knight, *Knight's Up-to-the-Minute Illustrations*, (Chicago: Moody Press, second printing, 1977) p. 74.

the heart becomes a leaden weight that hangs painfully from its tender moorings, unable to dance with laughter or sing for with joy. As a poet has written:

> A heart that has lost the will to sing
> Is like a butterfly with a broken wing.

Then one day, God breaks His silence. The sun shines, a butterfly flutters, the birds sing, a friend smiles, a joke is told, and you laugh. Your heart regains its song. You see that the world is still there, and you're still a part of it. You know that you will be happy again.

The pain will always be there, in the private regions of the heart where love is nurtured and memories are cherished. But the pain is lightened by the realization that, though your body is gone from sight, the reality of your life remains. Your footprints on my heart bear testimony that you lived, that you exulted, that you achieved, that you cared—that you loved. Your footprints on other hearts continually surface and remind your father, your brother and me of the pride we share in having touched your life and having been touched by you. We will remember you every time we see a Boy Scout uniform; every time we see an Order of the Arrow dance; every time we watch the Summerall Guards at The Citadel execute their intricate drills; every time we see a doctor applying his skills lovingly and expertly to heal and to save.

We will grieve for you so long as we draw breath. But we will also strive and achieve and love and revel in this precious life that we have and that we shared with you for those 23 years.

Those who do not know how to weep with their whole hearts don't know how to laugh either. We who love you have wept for you with our whole hearts. Now, in your memory, we will laugh and be happy, because you want us to laugh and be happy, and because we appreciate you, admire you, respect you and love you.

## The Testimony Is in Your Footprints

May the God who smiled upon us when He sent you into our arms hold you tenderly in His until the day when we join you in eternal peace. Until then, we will cherish the footprints you left on our hearts.

Love,
Mama

# For Further
# Information

For information on Dr. Muriel O'Tuel's availability to speak at your next convention, conference, or seminar, or for questions regarding the purchase or this book or other products call or write:

Dr. Muriel O'Tuel and Associates
P. O. Box 509
North Myrtle Beach, SC 29597
~~(803)~~ 249-6903 or ~~248-3251~~.
843                    249-6553